Financial Capability and Asset Building with Diverse Populations

T0270787

Global economic recovery in the aftermath of the Great Recession has not been experienced equally: while the share of wealth owned by the richest 3% has grown, the share owned by the poorest 90% continues to decline, as reported by Oxfam in 2016. This wealth divide disproportionately affects racial and ethnic minority communities.

This book underscores the importance of financial capability and asset building (FCAB) practice, policy and research during a period when vulnerable populations face increasingly difficult economic and financial realities. At the same time, retrenchment and privatization of government-sponsored social services have eroded the safety net available for families experiencing poverty or near-poverty conditions. The proliferation of products and services available from both formal and informal financial institutions highlights the need to promote FCAB to avoid and/ or recover from financial difficulties, crises and poverty. The contributors to this book disseminate findings from interventions designed to increase financial knowledge, financial management and financial access across several vulnerable populations, including immigrant communities. Further, they demonstrate the need for culturally sensitive FCAB service delivery, considering opportunities and barriers posed by past and current life situations, experiences and environments experienced by different populations. The book is aimed at policymakers, researchers and practitioners who assist financially vulnerable people.

The chapters in this book were originally published as a special issue of the *Journal of Community Practice*.

Julie Birkenmaier is a Professor of Social Work at Saint Louis University, USA. Her current research focuses on financial capability and asset building, including financial access and financial inclusion.

Margaret Sherraden is Research Professor at Washington University in St. Louis and Emeritus Professor of Social Work at the University of Missouri-St. Louis, USA. Her current research focuses on adult and youth savings, financial capability and community economic development.

Jodi Jacobson Frey is Associate Professor of Social Work at the University of Maryland, USA. Her research focuses on workplace behavioral health, emphasizing mental health, substance use and suicide prevention.

Christine Callahan is Research Assistant Professor with the Financial Social Work Initiative at the University of Maryland, USA. Her research focuses on interventions that social workers can use to promote greater financial capability, especially in vulnerable, under-served populations.

Anna Maria Santiago is Professor of Social Work at Michigan State University, USA. Her research focuses on financial capability and asset building in low-income families, neighborhood effects on the health and well-being of low-income children, low-income housing and homeownership, foreclosures and predatory lending in the United States and international contexts.

Financial Capability and Asset Building with Diverse Populations

Improving Financial Well-Being in Families and Communities

Edited by
Julie Birkenmaier, Margaret Sherraden, Jodi Jacobson Frey, Christine Callahan and Anna Maria Santiago

LONDON AND NEW YORK

First published 2018 by Routledge

2 Park Square, Milton Park, Abingdon, Oxfordshire OX14 4RN
52 Vanderbilt Avenue, New York, NY 10017

Routledge is an imprint of the Taylor & Francis Group, an informa business

First issued in paperback 2020

British Library Cataloguing in Publication Data
A catalogue record for this book is available from the British Library

ISBN13: 978-0-8153-8514-1 (hbk)
ISBN13: 978-0-367-59291-2 (pbk)

Typeset in Minion Pro
by diacriTech, Chennai

Publisher's Note
The publisher accepts responsibility for any inconsistencies that may have arisen
during the conversion of this book from journal articles to book chapters, namely
the possible inclusion of journal terminology.

Disclaimer
Every effort has been made to contact copyright holders for their permission to
reprint material in this book. The publishers would be grateful to hear from any
copyright holder who is not here acknowledged and will undertake to rectify any
errors or omissions in future editions of this book.

Contents

CONTENTS

Citation Information

The chapters in this book were originally published in the *Journal of Community Practice*, volume 24, issue 4 (October–December 2016). When citing this material, please use the original page numbering for each article, as follows:

Introduction
Financial Capability and Asset Building: Building Evidence for Community Practice
Julie Birkenmaier, Margaret Sherraden, Jodi Jacobson Frey, Christine Callahan, and Anna Maria Santiago
Journal of Community Practice, volume 24, issue 4 (October–December 2016) pp. 357–367

Chapter 1
Building Financial Knowledge Is Not Enough: Financial Self-Efficacy as a Mediator in the Financial Capability of Low-Income Families
David W. Rothwell, Mohammad N. Khan, and Katrina Cherney
Journal of Community Practice, volume 24, issue 4 (October–December 2016) pp. 368–388

Chapter 2
Promoting Financial Capability of Incarcerated Women for Community Reentry: A Call to Social Workers
Cynthia K. Sanders
Journal of Community Practice, volume 24, issue 4 (October–December 2016) pp. 389–409

Chapter 3
Toward Culturally Sensitive Financial Education Interventions with Latinos
Liza Barros Lane and Suzanne Pritzker
Journal of Community Practice, volume 24, issue 4 (October–December 2016) pp. 410–427

Chapter 4

From Being Unbanked to Becoming Unbanked or Unbankable: Community Experts Describe Financial Practices of Latinos in East Los Angeles
Larissa A. Padua and Joanna K. Doran
Journal of Community Practice, volume 24, issue 4 (October–December 2016)
pp. 428–444

Chapter 5

Ethnic Differences in Financial Outcomes Among Low-Income Older Asian Immigrants: A Financial Capability Perspective
Yunju Nam, Jin Huang, and Eun Jeong Lee
Journal of Community Practice, volume 24, issue 4 (October–December 2016)
pp. 445–461

Chapter 6

Financial Knowledge and Behaviors of Chinese Migrant Workers: An International Perspective on a Financially Vulnerable Population
Zibei Chen and Catherine M. Lemieux
Journal of Community Practice, volume 24, issue 4 (October–December 2016)
pp. 462–486

For any permission-related enquiries please visit:
http://www.tandfonline.com/page/help/permissions

Notes on Contributors

Liza Barros Lane is a doctoral candidate in the Graduate College of Social Work at the University of Houston, USA. Her research is focused on the financial capability of documented and undocumented Latino immigrants with respect to how their financial knowledge and access to the financial system influence financial outcomes.

Julie Birkenmaier is a Professor of Social Work at Saint Louis University, USA. Her current research focuses on financial capability and asset building, including financial access and financial inclusion.

Christine Callahan is Research Assistant Professor with the Financial Social Work Initiative at the University of Maryland, USA. Her research focuses on interventions that social workers can use to promote greater financial capability, especially in vulnerable, under-served populations.

Zibei Chen is a doctoral candidate at the School of Social Work, Louisiana State University, USA. Her current research focuses on financial literacy and financial inclusion among vulnerable populations.

Katrina Cherney is a Ph.D. candidate at the School of Social Work, McGill University, Canada.

Joanna K. Doran is Assistant Professor at the School of Social Work, California State University, USA.

Jodi Jacobson Frey is Associate Professor of Social Work at the University of Maryland, USA. Her research focuses on workplace behavioral health, emphasizing mental health, substance use and suicide prevention.

Jin Huang is an Associate Professor at the School of Social Work, College for Public Health and Social Justice, Saint Louis University, USA.

Mohammad N. Khan is a Ph.D. candidate at the School of Social Work, McGill University, Canada.

Eun Jeong Lee is the National SCSEP Director at the National Asian Pacific Center on Aging, USA.

Catherine M. Lemieux is Margaret Champagne Womack Professor in Addictive Disorders at the School of Social Work, Louisiana State University, USA.

Yunju Nam is Associate Professor at the School of Social Work, University at Buffalo, The State University of New York, USA.

Larissa A. Padua is a social worker with extensive experience working with low-income, immigrant families, and adults living with disabilities. She earned her Masters Degree in Social Work from California State University, Los Angeles, and is currently a research assistant at the University of Victoria, Canada. Her research interests include education and financial capability of vulnerable populations.

Suzanne Pritzker is Associate Professor at the Graduate College of Social Work, University of Houston, USA.

David W. Rothwell is Assistant Professor at the College of Public Health and Human Sciences, Oregon State University, USA.

Cynthia K. Sanders is Professor and MSW Program Coordinator at the School of Social Work, Boise State University, USA.

Anna Maria Santiago is Professor of Social Work at Michigan State University, USA. Her research focuses on financial capability and asset building in low-income families, neighborhood effects on the health and well-being of low-income children, low-income housing and homeownership, foreclosures and predatory lending in the United States and international contexts.

Margaret Sherraden is Research Professor at Washington University in St. Louis and Emeritus Professor of Social Work at the University of Missouri-St. Louis, USA. Her current research focuses on adult and youth savings, financial capability and community economic development.

Financial Capability and Asset Building: Building Evidence for Community Practice

Community practitioners have long been involved in helping clients manage their household finances and gain financial capability and build assets (Cruce, 2001; Stuart, 2013). Toward these ends, practitioners work in diverse community-based organizations to assist clients to acquire, maintain, and manage income; obtain education and training to enter the workforce; acquire and maintain employment; manage their finances; and many other direct services. Informed by their first-hand experience with clients, they also develop and direct workforce development, financial management, and asset development programs; evaluate their work; and disseminate their findings to other practitioners. Many household financial problems are rooted in systemic forces, such as poverty, discrimination, and poorly designed and unsafe financial products (Karger, 2015). Practitioners, therefore, also advocate in local communities for affordable and appropriate financial products, as well as empower and mobilize financially vulnerable people and communities to engage in policy practice to advance favorable social conditions, such as a higher minimum wage and affordable, accessible healthcare so that families can become more financially stable and secure.

The diverse work just described occurs within the context of communities comprised of working families challenged by today's financial realities. America's working households are struggling with low financial security (Wiedrich, Sims, Weisman, Rice, & Brooks, 2016). Despite an economy in the United States and globally that has largely recovered from the Great Recession, the majority of US households are facing their own increasingly difficult economic and financial realities. At the national level, the United States is experiencing extraordinary income and wealth inequality (Pew Research Center, 2015; Piketty, 2014; Saez & Zucman, 2014). This means that most of the income and wealth produced is going to the most affluent households (Pew Research Center, 2015), and the majority of US households hold a decreasing share of all income and wealth produced in the economy. Almost half of all income produced in 2014 went to upper-income households (i.e., those earning over $144,251 for a family of 4), an increase from 29% in 1970 (Pew Research Center, 2015). The share of income that went to middle-income households (i.e., those earning between $48,083 to 144, 251) was 43%, down from 62% in 1970 (Pew Research Center, 2015). In fact, family incomes adjusted for inflation have changed little over the past 3 to 4 decades (DeNavas-Walt & Proctor, 2014; Piketty & Saez, 2003). The trend of income concentration with the wealthiest is also true of assets—the share of all wealth owned by the richest 3% has grown, but the share owned by the poorest 90% has declined since 1989 (Bricker et al., 2014). These trends add up to a decline in the number of middle-class adults. From 2000 to 2014, over 200 US metropolitan areas experienced a decrease of middle-income adults (Pew Research Center, 2016).

The growing income and wealth divide has a strong racial component. Since 1986, White families have seen their average wealth grow by 84%—1.2 times the rate of growth for Latinos and three times the rate of growth for Black households. If the average Black family wealth grows at the same pace in the future as it has over the past 30 years, it will take 228 years for Black families to have the same amount of current average wealth of White families; it will take the average Latino family 84 years (Asante-Muhammed, Collins, Hoxie, & Nieves, 2016). These statistics clearly illustrate how wealth inequality in the United States is acutely experienced in communities of color.

The current community practice context in the United States is one of increasing poverty and decreasing political and social support for public programs. The current official poverty rate of 15% is higher than in 2007, the year prior to the Great Recession (DeNavas-Walt & Proctor, 2015). The number of families living in extreme poverty, with $2/person/day or less to spend on necessities, has doubled since the passage of welfare reform in 1996 (Edin & Shaefer, 2015). At the same time, government-sponsored human services have undergone retrenchment and privatization, resulting in a smaller and less secure safety net for families experiencing poverty or near-poverty conditions (Abramovitz & Zelnick, 2015). Thus, families have little to fall back on when they most need it, and little to help them get ahead financially. In fact, one in three American households have no savings at all, which makes them highly vulnerable in financial emergencies (Wiedrich et al., 2016).

The stakes of financial capability and asset building (FCAB) practice, policy, and research have never been higher. In addition to difficult economic conditions of stagnant wages, growing poverty, and a shrinking middle-class (Weil, Reisch, & Ohmer, 2013), today's financial context is more complicated than in previous generations. There are myriad financial products and services available from both formal financial institutions (such as banks and credit unions) and informal institutions (such as check-cashing stores). With fewer employer-sponsored retirement plans and pensions, people also have greater responsibility for making their own financial decisions that have long-term ramifications (Butrica, Iams, Smith, & Toder, 2009). The growth in individual responsibility, dovetailing with the growth in financial products and services, including those in the alternative financial services sector, has resulted in households needing to make higher-risk financial decisions. There is growing recognition that people need stronger financial capability and assets to avoid and recover from financial difficulties, crises, and poverty (Mitchell & Lusardi, 2015).

Local communities are where these challenging financial and economic trends and subsequent issues take form. Financial insecurity leaves families more prone to experiencing difficulty locating stable, affordable housing, and being food insecure (Desmond, 2015). Financial insecurity and instability leads to less participation in basic medical care, which results in lower life expectancy (Wiedrich et al., 2016). Poor family economic conditions have a negative impact on the material and social resources available to children, which negatively affect their earnings and health outcomes later in life (Holzer, Schanzenbach, Duncan, & Ludwig, 2008; Waldfogel, 2013). Children living in poverty often experience disruptions in their housing, and resulting disturbances in their academics as they change schools often, resulting in potential long-reaching ramifications for their life opportunities and career aspirations (Holzer et al., 2008; Waldfogel, 2013). Research has demonstrated that wealth and income disparities and their accompanying stress also have social effects that impact communities. Great disparities in wealth lead to higher levels of social distrust and breed cynicism in society (Wilkinson & Pickett, 2010). The perception of one's ability to move up the economic ladder within their community is imperative to an individual's efforts toward that end: low-income youth, especially boys, are more likely to drop out of school in communities with a larger income gap, which contributes to generational cycles of economic disadvantage (Kearney & Levine, 2016).

FCAB work aims to improve financial well-being in families and communities. Building on Nussbaum's (2011) capabilities approach, financial capability consists of both the *internal capabilities*, such as the individual's knowledge, skills and attitudes about finances, and *external conditions*, such as financial institutions (i.e., banks and credit unions), financial products and services (e.g., saving and checking accounts), and policy related to financial services and financial consumer protection. The combination of internal capabilities and external conditions facilitates an individual's ability to make informed financial decisions and perform financial behaviors that promote financial well-being, such as saving money on a regular basis and avoiding unnecessary fees (Sherraden, 2013). FCAB, as a concept, rests on the assumption that individuals have varying levels of financial capability due to both their internal capabilities and the external conditions present (or absent) in their communities, including the presence or dearth of financial products and services and resources available within their communities. Theory suggests that social interventions to improve FCAB focus on building internal capabilities through financial education efforts and changing external conditions through financial access and policy (Beverly, Clancy, & Sherraden, 2014; Huang, Nam, & Sherraden, 2013; Huang, Nam, Sherraden & Clancy, 2015; Sherraden, Frey, & Birkenmaier, 2016).

The growing number of financially vulnerable households has changed the landscape of community practice. As Mimi Abramovitz (2015) has noted, community practitioners are now working with three types of people who are poor: the *traditionally poor* who cannot work because of their age, disability status, or inability to find work; the *working poor* who are employed without pensions, benefits, and union protection; and the *new poor*, the former middle class who are facing stagnant wages and a jobless economic recovery. In today's practice environment, community practitioners often struggle to provide sufficient time to economically distressed clients to build the trust needed to effectively work with them on complex financial and economic problems (Abramovitz & Zelnick, 2015). Within this context, FCAB work is needed at all client systems levels, from direct practice to policy work to the fight for economic justice (Abramovitz, 2015).

In addition to practice interest, there is also growing academic and public policy interest in helping people gain financial capability and assets. Researchers are testing financial capability interventions with adults, children, immigrant populations, and other groups (Batty, Collins, & Odders-White, 2015; Huang et al., 2013; Robertson & Curley, 2016; Theodos et al., 2015). For example, interventions to help parents learn to save money include financial education and access to a college savings account (Huang et al., 2013). Policymakers are showing increased interest in interventions, and implementing new policies designed to increase financial capability and assets for the financially vulnerable households. For example, the states of Maine and Nevada have started statewide FCAB programs (Clancy, Sherraden, & Beverly, 2015). Even a few countries are creating national strategies on financial capability (Bagwell, Hestbaek, Harries, & Kail, 2014; Kempson, 2009). Yet more is needed.

It is within this context that a convening was held of FCAB scholars during the Spring of 2015. The purpose of the convening was to develop and hone a social work agenda in FCAB. The gathering of over 60 scholars was hosted by the Center for Social Development at the Brown School at Washington University in St. Louis, and the Financial Social Work Initiative at the School of Social Work at the University of Maryland, Baltimore. Wells Fargo Advisors and The Arthur Vining Davis Foundations provided funding for the meeting, and, together with The Woodside Foundation, supported the development of research manuscripts presented. This first-ever convening of its type represented a milestone event for community- and network-building among scholars researching FCAB topics.

This special issue of *JCP* features articles presented at the convening, and contributes toward the building of a body of research informing FCAB work in low-income communities and with financially vulnerable populations. The six convening articles presented in this issue examine important research questions for FCAB community practice and inform future research and practice efforts. They analyze the relationships among financial knowledge, financial self-efficacy, and savings outcomes to financial capability. They also consider the importance of cultural relevance in programs to promote financial capability to various populations and community settings. Other papers at the convening (published elsewhere) discussed questions related to FCAB and social work education and, more broadly, social work practice.

This special issue begins by examining the relationships among internal components of financial capability relative to financial behavior. In the first article, David W. Rothwell, Mohammed N. Khan, and Katrina Cherney tackle this question among low-income households in "Building financial knowledge is not enough: Financial self-efficacy as a mediator in the financial capability of low-income families." Using a national sample of low-income Canadians, they investigate relationships among financial knowledge, financial self-efficacy, and savings outcomes. Their results suggest that financial self-efficacy fully mediates the relationship between objective financial knowledge and post-secondary education saving. This finding, which underscores the relationship between people's feelings about their financial competence and their financial behaviors, suggests that financial capability program efforts focused on internal factors need to emphasize financial self-efficacy in addition to financial knowledge.

The articles that follow address the financial capability of incarcerated women, Latinos, older Asian immigrants, and migrant Chinese workers. Each underscores the importance of culturally relevant research and practice in FCAB work. Current measurement of financial literacy and capability may not be responsive to the financial experiences and environments of the various populations studied in these papers, such as Asian immigrant populations. Instead of employing a one-size-fits-all strategy, interventions and measurement of financial education and capability concepts must respond to the needs and circumstances of specific subpopulations. Community practitioners involved in FCAB work must collaborate with direct practitioners, community members belonging to the population of focus, and other professionals and policy leaders who can inform program design and delivery for financial capability work that best reflects the life experiences and unique aspects of that population.

Starting with FCAB among incarcerated women, Cynthia K. Sanders, in "Promoting financial capability of incarcerated women for community reentry: A call to social workers," focuses her research on this growing population. Women are the fastest growing correctional population in the United States, having increased 14 fold between 1970 and 2014 (Swavola, Riley, & Subramanian, 2016). The majority of incarcerated women are impoverished single mothers who are serving sentences for nonviolent drug-related and property offenses. Upon release, they face the hurdle of financial instability when trying to rebuild and stabilize their lives. Poverty, unemployment, and low incomes are all related to women's high rate of recidivism. This study contributes to the sparse literature on this topic by providing descriptive results of a financial education program with women incarcerated in a minimum-security prison. The instructors tailored the curriculum to the financial needs of the women both while incarcerated and after release, such as budgeting lessons relevant for their time pre- and postrelease. Findings indicate that women gained financial knowledge from the class experience that they can use on their postrelease financial choices. Because many crimes that women commit are money-related, economically empowering women may help to reduce the risk of recidivism. Sanders calls for additional financial capability programming and research with incarcerated women to improve their economic well-being after they are released.

Articles by Liza Barros Lane and Suzanne Pritzker, and Larissa A. Padua and Joanna K. Doran focus on Latinos, the largest minority population in the United States (US Census Bureau, 2015a). This population also faces major barriers to financial well-being, including, but not limited to the fact that 20% of the US Latino population is unbanked, with no relationship to a bank or credit union (FDIC, 2014). In the first article, "Toward culturally sensitive financial education interventions with Latinos," Barros Lane and Pritzker make the case that culturally sensitive interventions that attempt to build the financial knowledge and well-being of Latinos are needed. They find few peer-reviewed studies about financial education interventions to improve financial outcomes for Latinos and suggest that more research is needed to build a body of knowledge in this area. Using Resnicow et al.'s (1998) cultural sensitivity framework, surface methods of tailoring financial education (such as translating materials) and deep structure methods (such as acknowledging differences about financial services among countries) were identified, and have implications for designing and testing culturally sensitive financial education interventions. The authors suggest that the interventions should include deep structure methods, such as teaching financial information in the audience's first language, using instructors who are relatable to the audience, engaging the whole family in instruction, and using home-based instruction, such as financial education delivered through Spanish-language soap operas (i.e., telenovelas).

In the second article that focuses on the Latino experience, Padua and Doran provide answers to the question about which external conditions promote financial capability among Latinos in, "From being unbanked to becoming unbanked or unbankable: Community experts describe financial practices of Latinos in East Los Angeles." Using qualitative methods, they explore the cultural fit between financial structures and Latinos. Community experts were interviewed regarding financial practices in the predominantly low-income Latino and immigrant community of East Los Angeles, CA. Results suggest that, among Latinos, community mistrust passed through social networks and low financial education levels fuel fears of using formal financial institutions. Using informal financial institutions and limited financial education creates problems, such as problem debt or low credit scores, which result in Latinos making financial mistakes and becoming unbankable. The mistrust and lack of education (or miseducation) passed through social networks in this community calls for a comprehensive policy and practice approaches to build community trust and financial knowledge among the residents. Examples include incorporating financial literacy education within the local school system, creating safe and affordable financial products aimed at this population, and incentivizing saving.

Yunju Nam, Jin Huang, and Eun Jeong Lee provide the first empirical study of the role of financial capability on financial outcomes among Asian Americans, the fastest growing minority group in the United States (US Census Bureau, 2015b). Their article, "Ethnic differences in financial outcomes among low-income older Asian immigrants: A financial capability perspective," reports on financial outcomes among ethnic immigrant participants in a subsidized employment program. Findings show significant ethnic differences among older Chinese, Korean, and "Other Asian" participants in the financial outcomes of owning a bank account, long-term savings, and a credit card, and confidence in meeting basic expenses postretirement after controlling for financial capability and other factors. Factors related to participants' experience as ethnic minorities explain some of the observed differences in financial outcomes, such as saving regularly and building assets. The authors also suggest the need to develop culturally suitable financial capability measures for future research with older Asian populations to account for different financial experiences in their countries of origin; the influence of ethnic mass media and ethnic communities on financial activities, and access to ethnic banks and informal financial institutions (e.g., rotating saving and credit associations).

The special issue concludes with a discussion of FCAB concerns in a very different national context with Zibei Chen and Catherine M. Lemieux's article, "Financial knowledge and behaviors of Chinese migrant workers: An international perspective on a financially vulnerable population." Using survey data they collected, they found low levels of both financial knowledge and beneficial financial behaviors, such as financial record-keeping, budgeting, making ends meet, and saving retirement and emergencies, among Chinese rural-to-urban migrant workers. Those who were more knowledgeable about effective financial management, such as saving and borrowing and investment and risk, were more likely to engage in beneficial financial behaviors. Financial behaviors also were explained by financial attitudes, such as the importance of managing even small amounts of money, and socio-demographic characteristics (e.g., marital status and income). Their findings underscore the importance of culturally relevant educational interventions with low-paid migrant workers in China.

Taken together, these articles provide evidence to guide FCAB practitioners in their efforts to provide community interventions and further develop the field, as well as to FCAB scholars for future research. Much more work is needed to pilot, test, and disseminate results from interventions designed to increase financial knowledge, financial management, and financial access. To advance the field, interventions designed to address internal capability should include financial self-efficacy components (Rothman, Khan, & Cherney, 2016) that help participants gain both an appreciation for their knowledge and skills as well as self-confidence. Interventions must also be culturally sensitive to the population (Sanders; Padua & Doran; Barros Lane & Pritzker, 2016; Nam et al., 2016; Chen & Lemieux, 2016), taking into consideration the opportunities and barriers posed by past and current life situations, experiences, and environments of the population in the curricular content. Culturally sensitive FCAB interventions should include different delivery formats, presenters, concepts, and expectations than FCAB interventions designed for a general public. Regarding external conditions, formal financial institutions must work to enhance consumer trust by providing culturally sensitive products and services with low cost; offer services to undocumented people; and help all traditionally unbanked communities gain a financial foothold to build the demand for their products (Padua & Doran, 2016). Researchers should endeavor to create new and population-specific financial capability measures to expand the understanding of financial well-being across different population groups (Nam, Huang, & Lee, 2016). Such measures would take into account the possibility that some population groups may have had good reason to avoid formal financial institutions in the past and, therefore, may not have a good understanding of these systems, while recognizing that they may have manifested positive financial management in other ways (e.g., informally budgeted, balanced income and expenses, engaged in rotating saving and credit associations, saved cash at home, and paid bills on time).

We hope that this special issue provides ideas and suggestions about the development of FCAB within community practice. The articles selected for this issue illustrate important considerations of the challenges and opportunities for FCAB policy, practice, and research. We hope that it serves to inspire policymakers, researchers, and practitioners to forge ahead in their respective endeavors with new evidence and ideas about how to assist financially vulnerable people get ahead.

Acknowledgments

The authors thank The Woodside Foundation, Wells Fargo Advisors, and the Arthur Vining Davis Foundation for supporting the development of manuscripts presented at the 2015 Convening on Financial Capability and Asset Building. We also are deeply grateful for the many people who contributed their time and ideas to the convening and this special issue. We are developing a community of scholars, researchers, and practitioners who are helping the field move forward. We especially appreciate the support, time, intellectual energy, and expertise of the following special issue reviewers for their thoughtful critiques and suggestions that strengthened the articles included this special issue: Steven Anderson, David Ansong, Mahasweta Banerjee, J. Michael Collins, Jami Curley, Elena Delavega, Mathieu Despard, Terri Friedline, Leah Gjertson, Jennifer Greenfield, David Hodge, Jin Huang, Minchao Jin, Seon Mi Kim, TK Logan, Vernon Loke, Donncha Marron, Amanda Mathisen, Matthew Painter, Sherrie L. W. Rhine, Britt Rios-Ellis, Alicia Rodriguez de Rubio, Soonhee Roh, Megan Stanton, Deborah Svoboda, Patrick Wightman, Jing Jian Xiao, Qingwen Xu, Karen Zurlo

Julie Birkenmaier, Ph.D.
St. Louis University

Margaret Sherraden, Ph.D.
University of St. Louis-Missouri

Jodi Jacobson Frey, Ph.D.
University of Maryland, Baltimore

Christine Callahan, Ph.D.
University of Maryland, Baltimore

Anna Maria Santiago, Ph.D.
Michigan State University

References

Abramovitz, M. (2015). *Opening plenary*. St. Louis, Missouri: The Financial Capabilities Asset Building (FCAB) Conference. Presented April 15-17, 2015.

Abramovitz, M., & Zelnick, J. (2015). Privatization in the human services: Implications for direct practice. *Clinical Social Work Journal, 43*, 283–293. doi:10.1007/s10615-015-0546-1

Asante-Muhammed, D., Collins, C., Hoxie, J., & Nieves, E. (2016, August). *The ever-growing gap: Without change, African-American Latino families won't match white wealth for centuries*. Washington, DC: Corporation for Enterprise Development. Retrieved from http://cfed.org/policy/federal/The_Ever_Growing_Gap-CFED_IPS-Final.pdf

Bagwell, S., Hestbaek, C., Harries, E., & Kail, A. (2014). *Financial capability strategy for the UK: Financial capability outcome frameworks*. London, UK: New Philanthropy Capital. Retrieved from http://socialwelfare.bl.uk/subject-areas/services-activity/poverty-benefits/newphilanthropycapital/170409Financial-Capability-Outcome-Frameworks-MAS.pdf

Batty, M., Collins, J. M., & Odders-White, E. (2015). Experimental evidence on the effects of financial education on elementary school students' knowledge, behavior, attitudes. *Journal of Consumer Affairs, 49*, 69–96. doi:10.1111/joca.12058

Beverly, S. G., Clancy, M., & Sherraden, M. (2014). *Testing universal college savings accounts at birth: Early research from SEED for Oklahoma Kids*. CSD Research Summary No.14-08. St. Louis, MO: Washington University, Center for Social Development. Retrieved from http://cfed.org/assets/pdfs/SEED_OK_Hout.pdf

Bricker, J., Dettling, L. J., Henriques, A., Hsu, J. W., Moore, K. B., Sabelhaus, J. … Windle, R. A. (2014). Changes in U.S. family finances from 2010 to 2013: Evidence from the Survey of Consumer Finance. *Federal Reserve Bulletin, 100*, 10.

Butricia, B. A., Iams, H. M., Smith, K. E., & Toder, E. J. (2009). The disappearing defined benefit pension its potential impact on the retirement incomes of Baby Boomers. *Social

Security Bulletin, 69(3). Retrieved from https://www.ssa.gov/policy/docs/ssb/v69n3/v69n3p1.html

Clancy, M. M., Sherraden, M., & Beverly, S. G. (2015). *College savings plans: A platform for inclusive progressive Child Development Accounts.* CSD Policy Brief 15-07. St. Louis, MO: Center for Social Development, Washington University. Retrieved from http://csd.wustl.edu/Publications/Documents/PB15-07.pdf

Cruce, A. (2001). *A history of progressive-era school savings banking, 1870-1930* (Working Paper No. 01-3). St Louis, MO: Washington University, Center for Social Development. Retrieved from https://csd.wustl.edu/Publications/Documents/WP01-03_70.AHistoryOfProgressiveEraSchool.pdf

DeNavas-Walt, C., & Proctor, B. D. (2014). *Income poverty in the United States: 2013* (Current Population Reports, P60-249). Washington, DC: U.S. Census Bureau. Retrieved from https://www.census.gov/content/dam/Census/library/publications/2014/demo/p60-249.pdf

DeNavas-Walt, C., & Proctor, B. D. (2015, September). *Income poverty in the United States: 2014* (Current Population Reports, P60-252). Washington, DC: U.S. Census Bureau. Retrieved from https://www.census.gov/content/dam/Census/library/publications/2015/demo/p60-252.pdf

Desmond, M. (2015). *Unaffordable America: poverty, housing, eviction. fast focus* (p. 22). Madison, WI: University of Wisconsin-Madison, Institute for Research on Poverty. Retrieved from http://www.irp.wisc.edu/publications/fastfocus/pdfs/FF22-2015.pdf

Edin, K. J., & Shaefer, H. L. (2015). *$2.00 a day: Living on almost nothing in America.* Boston, MA: Houghton Mifflin Harcourt.

Federal Deposit Insurance Corporation [FDIC]. (2014). *2013 FDIC national survey of unbanked underbanked households.* Washington, DC: Author.

Holzer, H. J., Schanzenbach, D. W., Duncan, G. J., & Ludwig, J. (2008). The economic costs of childhood poverty in the United States. *Journal of Children Poverty, 14,* 41–61. doi:10.1080/10796120701871280

Huang, J., Nam, Y., Sherraden, M., & Clancy, M. (2015). Financial capability asset accumulation for children's education: Evidence from an experiment of child development accounts. *Journal of Consumer Affairs, 49,* 127–155. doi:10.1111/joca.2015.49.issue-1

Huang, J., Nam, Y., & Sherraden, M. S. (2013). Financial knowledge child development account policy: A test of financial capability. *Journal of Consumer Affairs, 47,* 1–26.

Karger, H. (2015). Curbing the financial exploitation of the poor: Financial literacy social work education. *Journal of Social Work Education, 51,* 425–438.

Kearney, M., & Levine, P. (2016). *Income inequality, social mobility, the decision to drop out of high school.* Washington, DC: Brookings Institution. Retrieved from http://www.brookings.edu/about/projects/bpea/papers/2016/kearney-levine-inequality-mobility

Kempson, E. (2009). Framework for the development of financial literacy baseline surveys: A first international comparative analysis. *OECD Working Papers on Finance, Insurance Private Pensions,* (1), 0_1. doi:10.1787/5kmddpz7m9zq-en

Mitchell, O., & Lusardi, A. (2015). *Financial literacy economic outcomes: Evidence policy implication* (Working paper). Retrieved from http://gflec.org/wpcontent/uploads/2015/06/LusardiMitchell_FInLitEconOutcomes6-4-15-Forthcoming-in-Journal-of-Retirement.pdf

Nussbaum, M. C. (2011). *Creating capabilities: The human development approach.* Cambridge, Massachusetts and London, England: The Belknap Press of Harvard University Press.

Pew Research Center. (2015). *The American middle class is losing ground: No longer the majority falling behind financially.* Washington, D.C.: Author. Retrieved from http://www.pewsocialtrends.org/files/2015/12/2015-12-09_middle-class_FINAL-report.pdf

Pew Research Center. (2016). *America's shrinking middle class: A close look at changes within metropolitan areas*. Washington, DC: Author. Retrieved from http://www.pewsocialtrends.org/2016/05/11/americas-shrinking-middle-class-a-close-look-at-changes-within-metropolitan-areas/

Piketty, T. (2014). *Capital in the twenty-first century*. Cambridge, MA: Harvard University Press.

Piketty, T., & Saez, E. (2003). Income inequality in the United States, 1913–1998. *Quarterly Journal of Economics, 118*, 1–41. doi:10.1162/00335530360535135

Resnicow, K., Baranowski, T., Ahluwalia, J. S., & Braithwaite, R. L. (1998). Cultural sensitivity in public health: Defined and demystified. *Ethnicity & Disease, 9*, 10–21.

Robertson, A. S., & Curley, J. (2016). *Annual report on the ASSET Project's Head Start Family Financial Capability Pilot* (CSD Research Report No. 16-04). St. Louis, MO: Washington University, Center for Social Development.

Saez, E., & Zucman, G. (2014). *Wealth inequality in the United States since 1913: Evidence from capitalized income tax data* (NBER Working Paper 20625. Cambridge, MA: National Bureau of Economic Research. Retrieved from http://www.nber.org/papers/w20625

Sherraden, M. S. (2013). Building blocks of financial capability. In J. M. Birkenmaier, M. S. Sherraden, & J. C. Curley (Eds.), *Financial capability asset building: Research, education, policy, practice* (pp. 3–43). New York, NY: Oxford University Press.

Sherraden, M. S., Frey, J. J., & Birkenmaier, J. M. (2016). Financial social work. In J. J. Xiao (Ed.), *Hbook of consumer finance* (2nd ed., pp. 115–130). New York, NY: Springer.

Stuart, P. H. (2013). Social workers financial capability in the profession's first half century. In J. M. Birkenmaier, M. S. Sherraden, & J. Curley's (Eds.), *Financial capability asset building: Research, education, policy, practice* (pp. 44–61). New York, NY: Oxford University Press.

Swavola, E., Riley, K., & Subramanian, R. (2016). *Overlooked: Women jails in an era of reform*. New York, NY: Vera Institute of Justice. Retrieved from https://www.vera.org/publications/overlooked-women–jails-report

Theodos, B., Simms, M., Treskon, M., Stacy, C., Brash, R., Emam, D., … Collazos, J. (2015). *An evaluation of the impacts implementation approaches of financial coaching programs*. Washington, DC: Urban Institute. Retrieved from http://www.urban.org/sites/default/files/alfresco/publication-pdfs/2000448 An Evaluation of the Impacts–Implementation-Approaches-of-Financial-Coaching-Programs.pdf

United States Census Bureau. (2015a). *FFF: Hispanic Heritage Month 2015*. Retrieved from http://www.census.gov/newsroom/facts-for-features/2015/cb15-ff18.html

United States Census Bureau. (2015b). *Projections of the size composition of the US Population: 2014 to 2060* Current Population Reports, P25-1143. Washington, DC: U.S. Census Bureau. Retrieved from https://www.census.gov/content/dam/Census/library/publications/2015/demo/p25-1143.pdf

Waldfogel, J. (2013). The safety net for families with children. In S. Danziger, & M. J. Bailey's (Eds.), *Legacies of the War on poverty* (pp. 153–178). New York, NY: Russell Sage Foundation.

Weil, M., Reisch, M., & Ohmer, M. L. (2013). Introduction: Contexts challenges for 21st century communities. In M. Weil, M. Reisch, & M. L. Ohmer (Eds.), *The handbook of community practice* (pp. 3–25). Thousand Oaks, CA: Sage.

Wiedrich, K., Sims, L.Jr.,, Weisman, H., Rice, S., & Brooks, J. (2016). *The steep climb to economic opportunity for vulnerable families*. Washington, DC: Corporation for Enterprise Development. Retrieved from http://assetsopportunity.org/assets/pdf/2016_Scorecard_Report.pdf

Wilkinson, R., & Pickett, K. (2010). *The spirit level: Why greater equality makes societies stronger*. New York, NY: Bloomsbury.

Building Financial Knowledge Is Not Enough: Financial Self-Efficacy as a Mediator in the Financial Capability of Low-Income Families

David W. Rothwell, Mohammad N. Khan, and Katrina Cherney

ABSTRACT

Policymakers in many countries have taken an interest in population-level financial capability. Limited empirical work has examined how constructs that makeup financial capability relate and how they function for individuals with low incomes. Using a national sample of low-income Canadians, we investigate relationships between financial knowledge, financial self-efficacy, and savings outcomes. Overall, we find that financial self-efficacy fully mediated the relationship between objective financial knowledge and postsecondary-education saving. The association between objective financial knowledge and retirement saving and emergency saving passed through financial self-efficacy. Efforts to promote financial capability need to focus on more than objective financial knowledge.

Social work—with its longstanding commitment to reducing poverty, in-depth understanding of the multilevel and systems affecting marginalized communities, and tradition of applied social research—is leading the scientific development and application of the theory of financial capability. Moreover, financial capability and asset building for all has been identified by the American Academy of Social Work and Social Welfare as one of the 12 grand challenges for social work in the 21st century (Sherraden et al., 2015). Financial capability consists of both the *internal capabilities*, such as knowledge, skills and attitudes, and *external conditions*, such as inclusive financial institutions and beneficial financial products and services. Together, internal capabilities and external conditions allow individuals to make informed financial decisions and perform desirable financial behaviors that contribute to their financial wellbeing (Sherraden, 2013). Underlying the theory is an assumption that individuals have varying levels of financial capability. Furthermore, to increase economic security on a broad scale, social interventions must improve both internal capabilities and external conditions.

To date, the relationships between the internal constructs that makeup financial capability theory have not been tested extensively and certainly not in a low-income sample. We address this gap by testing the relationships from a nationally representative survey of Canadians. The purpose of this article is to improve the understanding of how the internal constructs relate to each other and savings outcomes. We focus on financial self-efficacy as an understudied dimension of these internal abilities. The idea of self-efficacy, originally developed by Albert Bandura, suggests that all people seek to gain a sense of control over the events shaping their lives (Bandura, 1995). In a time of growing economic inequality and increasing complexity of financial choices, the ability to exercise command and control over financial resources has never been more complex. By refining the understanding of the mechanisms by which knowledge relates to behavior via self-efficacy, we help identify when and how community practice and economic development interventions might be more effective.

Background: financial capability and low-income saving

Policymakers in many countries are now interested in the concept of financial capability. The idea of financial capability originated from consumer finance and financial security scholars in the United Kingdom, led by Kempson and colleagues, who sought to understand the process of financial decision making. From the perspective of a rational consumer model, which implies that informed consumers make better financial decisions, Kempson, Collard, and Moore (2005) defined financial capability as the function of three interrelated components: financial knowledge, skills, and attitude. Later, emphasizing self-efficacy, De Meza, Irlenbusch, and Reyniers (2008) indicated that financial capability is determined more by individuals' psychological attributes, rather than simple possession of informational knowledge and skills. Informed by Sen's work on capabilities (Sen, 1999), social work scholars developed a model of financial capability in which they argued that people are financially capable when they possess "knowledge and competencies, ability to act on that knowledge, and opportunity to act" (Johnson & Sherraden, 2007, p. 122). Governments in Australia, Canada, Japan, the United States, and the United Kingdom now have state-led efforts to study and promote financial capability. Further, the Organization for Economic Co-operation and Development has initiated a cross-country effort to understand financial capability.

Several efforts are attempting to understand financial capability at the national level. However, there is considerable need to develop knowledge for how this model applies specifically to low-income groups. Studies and reports of financial capability show an expected income gradient for financial capability (Atkinson, McKay, Collard, & Kempson, 2007; Applied Research and Consulting LLC, 2009; Taylor, 2011). For example, the first national US study found that 83% of persons with over $75,000 in annual household income rated their financial knowledge high, compared to 56% of persons with household income less than $25,000 (Applied Research and Consulting LLC, 2009). A similar gradient was observed in a more objective five question assessment of money knowledge (average correct answers for low income group was 2.02 compared to 3.42 in the upper income group). Additional studies have suggested that financial knowledge and financial inclusion are associated with savings among low-income people (Huang, Nam, Sherraden, & Clancy, 2015; Jamison, Karlan, & Zinman, 2014). We are not aware of any national studies that examine the financial capability of only those at the bottom of the income distribution.

Conceptual framework

Our study is informed by the financial capability framework proposed by Sherraden (2013). In this framework, a key distinction is made between an individual's internal capabilities and external conditions, determined by the macro-economic environment (Sherraden, 2013). As mentioned, the primary purpose of this study is to examine relationships between the internal constructs that makeup financial capability and the behavioral outcome of saving.

A person's knowledge about financial systems and money markets is a necessary component of financial capability. Financial knowledge—an internal construct—is defined as an individual's understanding of both micro and macro economics and finance (Lusardi & Mitchell, 2014). More specifically, financial knowledge is comprised of (a) numeracy, (b) understanding inflation, and (c) understanding risk diversification. Previous studies use various terms to capture the idea of objective financial knowledge such as financial knowledge, financial literacy, and actual knowledge (Babiarz & Robb, 2014; Robb & Woodyard, 2011; Xiao, Chen, & Chen, 2014). For clarity, we use the term *objective financial knowledge.*

Objective financial knowledge—as with other forms of knowledge like reading and math—is measured through an assessment of answers to questions that are scored correct or incorrect (Lusardi & Mitchell, 2014), and is positively correlated with a number of saving and other positive financial behaviors (Hilgert, Hogarth, & Beverly, 2003). For example, a recent experiment showed the probability of holding a children's savings account was 8.7 percentage points higher for mothers with high levels of objective financial knowledge, compared to low objective financial knowledge (Huang, Nam, & Sherraden, 2013). Interventions to promote objective financial knowledge normally include an array of topics such as fundamentals of the financial system, interest, and credit management and take place in various social work and other settings, e.g., educational programs in high schools, community-based seminars and workshops.

A sense of control and confidence in financial matters is also an essential internal component of financial capability. We refer to this as *financial self-efficacy*. The construct of financial self-efficacy is a subjective indicator of financial capability, and is rooted in the original theoretical developments of self-efficacy (Bandura, 1982). Financial self-efficacy is understood as an individual's attitudes, beliefs, and confidence in making financial decisions (Kempson et al., 2005). Importantly, in conceptualization and measurement, financial self-efficacy is distinct from objective financial knowledge. People may be highly confident in their ability to manage finances but have relatively little objective knowledge, and vice-versa.

Financial self-efficacy has not been studied as extensively as objective financial knowledge, but existing literature shows positive relationships with economic outcomes. In the US national survey, an increase in financial self-efficacy was associated with an eight percentage point increase in the probability of emergency savings (Babiarz & Robb, 2014). Importantly, research has shown an empirical distinction between financial self-efficacy and objective financial knowledge (Danes & Haberman, 2007; Xiao et al., 2014). At present, an explicit focus on self-efficacy is not included in most interventions to build financial knowledge, although some programs are now experimenting with the idea (see e.g., Loke, Choi, & Libby, 2015).

The opportunity to act, an external condition, is the second component of Sherraden's (2013) financial capability framework. Opportunity to act is defined as access to financial products, services, and institutions and is a key feature that distinguishes financial capability from financial literacy. The opportunity to act is determined by the inclusiveness of institutions and the existence of beneficial financial services and products (Sherraden, 2013). We acknowledge this feature of the financial capability theory; however, our study does not explicitly focus on how opportunity to act shapes savings outcomes.

Hypotheses

Social workers need to understand how the constructs that makeup financial capability theory are related. A relevant practice question is thus: to what extent should financial capability interventions focus on objective financial knowledge versus financial self-efficacy? To advance the theory of financial capability, this study tests three models of financial capability (see Figure 1). The first model, *direct*, hypothesizes that savings outcomes are directly and positively related to objective financial knowledge only (path *c*). In the second model, we hypothesize a *full mediation* model; i.e., objective financial knowledge relates to savings outcomes via financial self-efficacy (paths *a* and *b*). In model 3, we test the

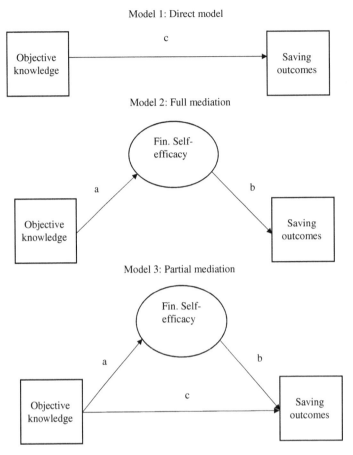

Figure 1. Hypothesized relationships between objective financial knowledge, financial self-efficacy and saving outcomes. Outcomes include (a) saving for education, (b) saving for retirement, and (c) $500 emergency savings.

proposition that financial self-efficacy "mediates the relationship between knowledge and action" (Bandura, 1982, p. 122). Model 3 is a *partial mediation* model that includes both the direct (c) and indirect paths (a and b). Our conceptual framework assumes, first, that objective financial knowledge is positively associated with saving behavior. The framework also assumes a second route of influence via financial self-efficacy and this, in turn, is also associated with saving behaviors. By systematically testing these three different paths, we gain specific knowledge about how the components of financial capability function. To our knowledge, no studies in the financial capability or financial literacy fields have examined the mediating role of financial self-efficacy, and almost certainly not among a nationally representative low-income sample. We control for, but do not examine, the influence of external conditions on financial knowledge or financial self-efficacy.

Method

Data

We accessed restricted data from Statistics Canada's 2009 Canadian Financial Capability Survey (CFCS) via the Statistics Canada Research Data Centre.[1] The CFCS is the only known nationally-representative data source that measures financial capability in Canada. The full sample consisted of 15,519 adult Canadians, representing 26.2 million residents of Canada aged 18 and older in 2009. Interviews were conducted by telephone between February and May 2009. Although the large sample size allows for estimations at the national and provincial level, they are limited by exclusion of individuals without home telephones, and residents of institutions and of the Northern Territories. The overall response rate of the survey was 56.3% (Statistics Canada, 2009). Weights were used to adjust for item nonresponse, bias for selecting one individual in the household, and inconsistency in province-age-sex ratios with population estimates projected in the most recent Canadian Census.

Canadian context

Canada's unique set of saving policy incentives have considerable implications for asset-building policymakers and practitioners in the United States (Lewis & Elliott, 2014). Regarding the financial landscape, Canada has federally-regulated, tax-preferred education and retirement savings vehicles. In terms of education savings, government incentives in Canada are more pervasive and generous, and families are accessing them at much higher rate than in the United States. However, in both countries, families with higher income, education and wealth are more likely to use these savings vehicles.

Measurement

Using the conceptual framework outlined previously, we aim to understand how the components of financial capability relate to each other and to saving.

Savings

Savings are a type of financial asset that can be used to smooth consumption during difficult times and promote future development (Sherraden, 1991). We selected three savings outcomes as dependent variables. The first asked whether or not the individual was saving for children's postsecondary education. The second asked about saving for retirement. And, the third asked about emergency savings. All binary variables were scored as 1 = *presence of saving* and 0 = *absence*. Whereas saving for children's education and retirement planning have major intergenerational and life course implications, emergency saving is an indicator of financial security (Gjertson, 2015).

Component 1: objective financial knowledge

The CFCS survey included a 14-item multiple-choice scale to assess objective financial knowledge. These items were derived from an earlier 8-item money quiz used in the first 2005 national UK survey of financial capability (Kempson & Collard, 2006). The questionnaire design underwent two rounds of cognitive testing and revisions before full-scale implementation (Statistics Canada, 2009). Items were scored correct or incorrect. A sample question reads, "If the inflation rate is 5% and the interest rate you get on your savings is 3%, will your savings have at least as much buying power in a year's time?" The measure reported in the analysis was the sum value of correct items. Scores ranged from zero to 14, with a higher score indicating more knowledge (Chronbach's α = .69). The Appendix shows all items in the objective financial knowledge scale with unweighted responses.

Component 2: financial self-efficacy

We define financial self-efficacy as the subjective assessment of one's knowledge, skills and ability to manage and control one's household finances. Bandura (2006) explained that any measure of self-efficacy must be domain specific, focused on execution (rather than achievement) of function, comprehensive, graded, and reflect challenges associated with the domain. A five-item self-efficacy scale targeting the financial domain was created from the survey items. The scale included self-ratings on financial knowledge, keeping track of money, making ends meet, shopping for financial products, and staying informed (items and unweighted summaries are reported in the Appendix). Each response ranged from 1 to 4, with 1 corresponding to *very good* and 4 corresponding to *not very good*. Responses that indicated *don't' know, refusal,* or *not stated* were coded as missing. Each item was reverse-scored so that higher scores reflect higher financial self-efficacy. A summary score of financial self-efficacy was constructed with a range of 5 to 20. Cronbach's alpha for the original five items was .75, indicating acceptable reliability. In measuring efficacy in relation to several domains of financial decision-making (i.e., keeping track of money, shopping around for financial products, etc.), our scale of financial self-efficacy is broader than previous studies that used a single item (Babiarz & Robb, 2014; Xiao et al., 2014).

Covariates

Demographic and socio-economic variables that are correlated with savings outcomes were included as control variables. Categorical variables included gender, education, employment, immigration; continuous variables included age, household income,[2] and household size. We also control for external conditions by including provincial data on welfare eligibility asset limits and benefits levels (National Council of Welfare, 2010). In Canada, most social assistance policies are determined at the provincial level. Welfare eligibility asset limits are chosen as an indicator of opportunity to act under the assumption that low asset limits restrict the opportunity to save and accumulate assets. Several previous studies have sought to evaluate the effect of asset limits on saving behaviors (Hurst & Ziliak, 2006; Rice & Bansak, 2014; Sullivan, 2006). Furthermore, benefit levels indicate a province's general preference toward spending on the poor. In multilevel cross-national studies, welfare generosity was associated with reduced likelihood of single mother poverty (Brady & Burroway, 2012). In the provincial policy dataset, three family types are reported: single, no children; single with child; and two parent with children. Both asset limits and maximum benefits vary considerably from province to province (e.g., asset limits range from $50 in Prince Edward Island to $4,000 in Manitoba). To create the welfare index, a standardized score was generated from the two indicators (mean 0 and variance of 1), with higher scores indicating more welfare generosity (i.e., higher asset limits and higher levels of welfare benefits). For interpretation this index was simply rescaled on a range of 0 to 100.

Analysis

The full CFCS data was restricted in the following steps. First, we filtered the data to include the three family types available in the welfare policy dataset: single, no children; single parent with children, and two parents with children ($n = 8,663$). We then filtered the dataset to include only individuals 65 and under to focus on working-age adults resulting in an adjusted sample of $n = 6,518$. Third, we subsampled low-income households by using a relative poverty threshold (50% of median household income, adjusted for household size). Households below this low income threshold were retained in the analysis as the low income sample ($n = 1,408$).

The first step in the analysis was to describe the low-income sample. Next we conducted exploratory and confirmatory factor analysis for the financial self-efficacy measure. Finally, we analyzed three structural models for each of the three outcomes: post-secondary education savings (a), retirement savings (b), and emergency savings (c).[3] Because respondents resided within different provinces with various policy differences, standard errors were clustered at the province level and the subpopulation command adjusted for the subsample of low income. To test the hypotheses, we proceeded by comparing the three models in Figure 1 against each other. Furthermore, as Model 1 (direct) and Model 2 (full mediation) were nested within Model 3 (partial), we tested for differences across models using the difference in chi-square test. By assessing the fit of each model relative to the others we were able to

Table 1. Description of sample

	Low-income
Covariates	$n = 1{,}408$
Family type	
Single without children	39
Single with children	22
Couple with children	39
Gender	
Male	50
Education level	
Less than high school	22
High school	40
More than high school	38
Employment status	
Full time	61
Immigration status	
Canadian	72
Province (Welfare index)	
Newfoundland Lab (39.5)	2
Prince Edward Island (35.6)	0.6
Nova Scotia (29.7)	4
New Brunswick (26.6)	3
Quebec (34.3)	23
Ontario (35.7)	38
Manitoba (52.5)	5
Saskatchewan (40.6)	4
Alberta (34.3)	7
British Columbia (28.6)	14
Age	38.2 (11.1)
Household size	3.6 (1.8)
Income	28,000
Independent variables	
Financial self-efficacy†	12.4 (3.2)
Objective knowledge	8.0 (2.6)
Dependent variables	
Saving for education	52
Retirement planning	47
Emergency savings	87

Note. † This includes 5 items and ranges 5–20. Based on the factor analysis one of the items (ability to make ends meet) was dropped. Percentages reported. For continuous variables means reported with standard deviations in parentheses. The median value is reported for household income.

conclude which model fits the data best (i.e., we tested the hypotheses stated previously). All models included the full list of covariates presented in Table 1. Importantly, the structural models produced here are not causal and we are not suggesting that objective financial knowledge is causing financial self-efficacy or savings outcomes. Instead, our goal is to systematically examine the relationship between objective financial knowledge, financial self-efficacy and savings outcomes while statistically controlling for other factors. For the sake of parsimony, we report only the coefficients for objective financial knowledge, financial self-efficacy, and the outcomes. Full model results with coefficients for covariates are available upon request.

Results

A description of the sample appears in Table 1. The mean age was 38.2 (SD = 11.1) and was comprised of 50% male-headed households, and 61% full-time employed. Just under 40% were in single households without children and coupled households with children, respectively. A smaller minority (22%) were part of single-headed households with children. The provincial welfare index variable showed considerable variation, ranging from 26.6 in New Brunswick to 52.5 for Manitoba. Out of the 20-point scale mean financial self-efficacy was 12.4 (SD = 3.2). For objective financial knowledge the mean score was 8 of 14 items correct (SD = 2.6). On dependent variables, 52% of families with children were saving for higher education; 47% were saving for retirement and 13% had no emergency savings. In results not shown, financial self-efficacy and objective knowledge scores were lower in the low income sample compared to the population overall. Furthermore, the overall population was much more likely to save for education (76%), retirement (80%), and report emergency savings (98%).

Measurement model

Exploratory factor analysis (EFA) was used to assess the proposed dimensionality of the financial self-efficacy scale. A one-factor model was a better fit than a two-factor model. One item—perceived ability to make ends meet—was dropped due to a low factor loading (< .6). Detailed EFA results are available upon request. The measurement model was then tested using confirmatory factor analysis after the item was dropped. Based on the chi-squared test, root mean squared error of approximation (RMSEA), and comparative fit index (CFI), our revised measurement model of financial self-efficacy fit the data well, χ^2(2, N = 1328) = 17.330; p < .001; $RMSEA$ = .076; CFI = .979.

Hypothesis tests

The three hypothesized structural models (Model 1 direct; Model 2 full; Model 3 partial) were tested with MPlus using weighted least-squares with mean and variance adjustment (Muthén, Toit, & Spisic, 1997). The chi-squared difference test is used to compare a base model to a rival model. In our framework, models 1 and 2 are nested within the base model 3. Therefore, we used the chi-square difference test to evaluate model fits relative to model 3. Results of testing the three models across the three outcomes appear in Table 2. For postsecondary-education savings, model A1 (direct) showed that objective financial knowledge had little impact on saving for post-secondary education. In comparison, the full mediation model (model A2) was a better model fit, χ^2(24, N - 704) - 31.312;

Table 2. Results of model tests: direct, full mediation, and partial mediation.

Model	RMSEA (c.i.)	TLI /CFI	χ^2 (p)	$\Delta\chi^2$ (p)	N (df)	Std. coef.	Indirect
Post-sec. education saving							
Model A1: Direct effect	.043(.029, .056)	.557 /.683	68.43 (.001)	40.906 (.000)	704 (30)	–	–
Obj knowledge → dv						.038	
Model A2: Full mediation	.021(.000, .039)	.899 /.939	31.342 (.1442)	.187 (.6651)	704 (24)	–	–
Obj knowledge → F. self-eff						.101***	.026***
F. self-eff → dv						.256***	
Model A3: Partial mediation	.022(.000, .041)	.885 /.934	30.992 (.123)	–	704 (23)	–	
Obj. knowledge → F. self-eff						.098***	.025***
F. self-eff → dv						.254***	
Obj. knowledge → dv						.014	
Retirement planning							
Model B1: Direct effect	.036(.026, .045)	.631 /.723	78.717 (.000)	46.138 (.000)	1283 (30)	–	–
Obj knowledge → dv						.100**	
Model B2: Full mediation	.022(.006, .034)	.865 /.919	38.268 (.033)	7.31 (.007)	1283 (24)	–	–
Obj knowledge → F. self-eff						.077***	.012***
F. self-eff → dv						.151***	
Model B3: Partial mediation	.020(.000, .033)	.883 /.933	34.816 (.06)	–	1283 (23)	–	
Obj. knowledge → F. self-eff						.073***	.011***
F. self-eff → dv						.147***	
Obj. knowledge → dv						.089*	
Emergency savings							
Model C1: Direct effect	.037(.027, .046)	.608/.706	81.538(.000)	45.553 (.000)	1282 (30)	–	–
Obj knowledge → dv						.084***	
Model C2: Full mediation	.025(.012, .037)	.817/.89	43.124(.009)	8.403 (.004)	1282 (24)	–	–
Obj knowledge → F. self-eff						.082***	.016**
F. self-eff → dv						.190***	
Model C3: Partial mediation	.022(.007, .035)	.857/.918	37.472(.029)	–	1282 (23)	–	
Obj. knowledge → F. self-eff						.073***	.013**
F. self-eff → dv						.181***	
Obj. knowledge → dv						.070**	

Note. $* = p < .05$; $** = p < .01$; $*** = p < .001$.

$p = .1442$; $RMSEA = .021$; $CFI = .939$. In this model, a standard deviation increase in financial self-efficacy had a strong influence on education saving ($\beta = .256$; $p < .001$). Further, about 10% of that influence came through from objective financial knowledge via financial-self-efficacy (mediating influence, $\beta = .026$; $p < .001$). Model A3 (partial) showed similar to just slightly poorer model fit compared to model A2, χ^2 (23, $N = 704$) = 30.992; $p = .123$; $RMSEA = .022$; $CFI = .934$. Adding the direct path to the models did not improve the overall model fit. In other words, for postsecondary-education saving, Model 2 (full mediation) from Figure 1 is the relatively best way to interpret the relationships. Although we controlled for the influence of opportunity to act on post-secondary education savings, this relationship was not statistically significant.

In the second set of models, a standard deviation increase in objective financial knowledge was associated with a higher likelihood of retirement saving ($\beta = .100$; $p < .01$). In our comparison of the models, the partial mediation model B3 fit the data much better than the other two models, χ^2 (30, $N = 1283$) = 34.816; $p < .06$; $RMSEA = .02$; $CFI = .933$. In this model B3, both the direct path from objective financial knowledge to retirement planning and the indirect path via financial self-efficacy were statistically significant ($\beta = .089$; $p < .01$; $\beta = .147$; $p < .01$). Furthermore, the indirect influence via financial self-efficacy was also significant ($\beta = .011$; $p < .01$). As for the previous set of models, the index for opportunity to act was not related to retirement saving.

In the last set of models, objective financial knowledge was related to emergency savings ($\beta = .084$; $p < .001$). Comparative model fit indices suggest the third model C3 was the best fit of the model: model C1 vs. model C3, χ^2 difference(7, $N = 1282$) = 45.553; $p < .001$; model C2 vs. model C3, χ^2 difference(6, $N = 1282$) = 8.403; $p < .01$. In model C3, a standardized increase in objective financial knowledge was associated with an increase in probability of emergency saving ($\beta = .070$; $p < .001$). Also, there appears to be evidence for the mediating hypothesis, i.e., that objective financial knowledge influences emergency savings via financial self-efficacy ($\beta = .013$; $p < .01$). Again, the index for opportunity to act was not related to emergency saving.

Discussion

Amidst rising economic inequality, there is renewed interest in promoting the economic security of individuals and families. Previous studies have demonstrated that financial behaviors are not fully explained by financial knowledge. In this study, we use nationally representative Canadian data to investigate how the internal constructs of financial capability are related to savings behaviors for low-income individuals. More specifically, we tested (a) how objective financial knowledge is related to a range of savings outcomes,

(b) how financial self-efficacy is related to a range of savings outcomes, and (c) the extent to which financial self-efficacy mediates the influence of objective financial knowledge on savings outcomes. A number of key findings warrant further discussion in relation to community practice.

The importance of financial self-efficacy in the financial capability process is the major contribution of this study. Our findings corresponds with recent studies reporting similar findings (Loke et al., 2015; Xiao et al., 2014). We find that attitudes and perceptions about finances matter a great deal for understanding variation in saving outcomes. In effect, we provide evidence to support Bandura's (1982) claim that self-efficacy mediates the relationship between knowledge and action. The positive coefficients for financial self-efficacy were the most consistent and exhibited the largest effect sizes, even after controlling for household income and the opportunity to act. In the partial mediation models, ceteris paribus, a one standard deviation increase in financial self-efficacy score was associated with a standardized increase in the probability of education saving (.25), retirement planning (.15), and emergency saving (.18), respectively.

Practice implications

As financial markets and decisions become increasingly complex, social workers in a variety of settings can provide opportunities to develop financial self-efficacy. First, community interventions can explicitly incorporate experiential, group, and peer-to-peer activities to build confidence around financial matters. This recommendation is supported by our findings and a body of research suggesting benefits of experiential program components (Adams & West, 2015; Birkenmaier & Curley, 2009). Second, whenever possible, community practitioners can connect clients with safe and secure financial institutions. By *safe and secure*, we mean financial institutions that are not predatory. Community-based credit unions and institutions funded by the Community Development Financial Institutions Fund are examples of where safe and secure financial products are likely to be offered. Financial institution representatives can participate in the organization's activities on-site. Social workers can also connect clients to financial services indirectly. For example, social workers can share information and strategies about how to access certain account features in a given institution. The relationships between staff members and financial institution was viewed positively by participants in one recent study of emergency savings programs (Adams & West, 2015). Third, practitioners might explicitly program time and space to explore the meaning of financial capability. Some may consider this approach as financial coaching. For example, caseworkers can incorporate discussions of efficacy into using cash or in-kind assistance such as housing and utilities. The impact of a social situation, such as a community-based financial capability intervention, is largely dependent on the subjective meaning that each individual places on the situation (Ross & Nisbett, 1991). This is still a relatively unexplored area in financial capability interventions, with much to be learned about how clients perceive the social aspects of their efforts to become financially capable. In combination, we expect these three activities to promote a sense of financial self-efficacy.

Interventions are experimenting with how to build financial self-efficacy. MyPath in San Francisco is an example program targeting economically disadvantaged youth. Embedded in peer support is a focus on building self-perceptions and attitudes about finances. For instance, youth in the MyPath program build their confidence around financial management through exercising autonomy and communication skills and preliminary evaluation results show some positive outcomes (Loke et al., 2015). Although a number of innovations in practice exist, they tend to only reach small portions of the low income population. There is need for funders and governments to learn from service providers and to pilot promising programs at a larger scale.

Although the major finding is the mediating role of financial self-efficacy, we should also highlight the direct relationship between saving and objective financial knowledge. For both retirement planning and emergency savings, objective knowledge matters. Efforts to build financial knowledge remain important for community practice. How to teach financial knowledge is a contested topic, especially considering recent findings showing rather weak associations between financial education courses and positive behaviors (Fernandes, Lynch, & Netemeyer, 2014).

Policy implications

The Canadian government has demonstrated a commitment to increasing financial capability in the country. In 2014, under the Financial and Consumer Agency of Canada (FCAC), the country launched a National Strategy for Financial Literacy. The National Strategy aims to:

> mobilize and engage public, private, and non-profit sectors to strengthen the financial literacy of Canadians and empower them to achieve the following goals: (a) manage money and debt wisely; (b) plan and save for the future; and prevent and protect against fraud and financial abuse. (FCAC, 2016)

With funding from the Government of Canada's Social Development Partnerships Program, the Financial Empowerment Champions (FEC) Project is a concrete example of how the federal government aims to partner with financial institutions (TD Canada Trust) and nonprofits (Prosper Canada) to build financial capability. The FEC Project will fund several community organizations throughout the country to increase their financial knowledge, skills, and confidence of persons living on low incomes (Prosper

Canada, 2016). Financial coaching and the creation of financial action plans feature prominently in the FEC strategy. When it comes to saving for education, our findings suggest that FEC interventions focusing on financial self-efficacy, in addition to objective financial knowledge, may have the greatest potential to build savings.

Limitations

This cross-sectional design does not establish causal relationships. Other designs are needed to better control for unobserved within-individual characteristics. Although statistically significant relationships were observed for financial self-efficacy after controlling for income and other socio-economic factors, we note the magnitude of estimates are not extremely large. The largest estimates were about one-fourth of a standard deviation.

Whereas missing item-level data on the objective financial knowledge and financial self-efficacy measures reduced the low income sample ($n = 126$), we did not find any observable differences for those with missing data. Last, we tested only one direction of the relationships, i.e., that objective financial knowledge leads to financial self-efficacy. However, this relationship might very well go in the reverse direction or include other relationships not tested here. For example, one alternative framework might suggest that objective financial knowledge could lead to financial behaviors that then build financial self-efficacy. Testing different directions of influence and feedback loops should be considered in future structural models of financial capability.

Implications for research

At the individual level, future research is needed to better understand the relationships between objective financial knowledge, financial self-efficacy and savings outcomes. In this study, we use survey items to measure the constructs in the financial capability framework. The field would benefit from psychometric work in the future. For example, latent variable methods such as Item Response Theory might improve our understanding of the objective financial knowledge scale. In terms of outcomes, future research might extend how the financial capability constructs relate to the US Consumer Financial Protection Bureau's (CFPB) financial well-being scale (CFPB, 2015). At the community level, there is a great need to improve our understanding of the opportunity to act component. Specifically, opportunity to act was not related to savings outcomes for the low-income sample in this study. From this study, we are unable to conclude whether this is best explained by a misspecification of opportunity to act or the dependent variables, or if the framework as a whole is not supported by the data. Moving forward, we recommend testing different opportunity to act indicators such as geographic clustering of financial services, safe and secure access, proximity to a financial service provider, discrimination, and safety.

Conclusion

Increasing economic security is a priority for social work. Social workers play at least two important roles in shaping economic security: (a) developing and delivering interventions to build financial capability among marginalized groups, and (b) creating and modifying policy institutions that shape economic opportunity. In this study, we provide evidence from a nationally-representative Canadian sample of low-income households that the influence of objective financial knowledge on savings for post-secondary education is mediated by financial self-efficacy. As such, improving objective financial knowledge is necessary but not sufficient to build financial capability. Knowledge of financial systems, banking, interest, and credit will only take behavior so far. We suggest that interventions to promote financial self-efficacy and research to understand the impact of those interventions are important future directions for community practice.

Notes

1. Access to this data is highly protected by Statistics Canada. An application to use the data must be approved by Statistics Canada. Analysis of this data took place in a secure and locked laboratory on the campus of McGill University in Montreal. All results were carefully vetted by a Statistics Canada employee to ensure that privacy and anonymity were protected.
2. In the regression models, we use the natural log of household income to account for the skewed distribution.
3. For post-secondary education savings we restricted the sample to only households with children ($n = 704$).

References

Adams, D., & West, S. (2015). Asset building among low income adults: An exploratory study with participants in an emergency savings program. *Journal of Community Practice, 23*(3–4), 436–461. doi:10.1080/10705422.2015.1091421

Applied Research and Consulting LLC. (2009). *Financial capability in the United States: Initial report of research findings from the 2009 National Survey.* FINRA investor education foundation. Retrieved from http://www.finrafoundation.org/web/groups/foundation/@foundation/documents/foundation/p120536.pdf

Atkinson, A., McKay, S., Collard, S., & Kempson, E. (2007). Levels of financial capability in the UK. *Public Money & Management, 27*(1), 29–36. doi:10.1111/pmam.2007.27.issue-1

Babiarz, P., & Robb, C. A. (2014). Financial literacy and emergency saving. *Journal of Family and Economic Issues, 35*(1), 40–50. doi:10.1007/s10834-013-9369-9

Bandura, A. (1982). Self-efficacy mechanism in human agency. *American Psychologist, 37*(2), 122–147. doi:10.1037/0003-066X.37.2.122

Bandura, A. (1995). *Self-efficacy in changing societies* (A. Bandura Ed.). Cambridge, UK.: Cambridge University Press.

Bandura, A. (2006). Guide for constructing self-efficacy scales. In F. Pajares, & T. C. Urdan (Eds.), *Self-efficacy beliefs of adolescents* (pp. 307–337). Greenwich, CT: Information Age.

Birkenmaier, J., & Curley, J. (2009). Financial credit: Social Work's role in empowering low-income families. *Journal of Community Practice, 17*(3), 251–268. doi:10.1080/10705420903117973

Brady, D., & Burroway, R. (2012). Targeting, universalism, and single-mother poverty: A multilevel analysis across 18 affluent democracies. *Demography, 49*(2), 719–746. doi:10.1007/s13524-012-0094-z

Consumer Financial Protection Bureau. (2015). *Measuring financial well-being: A guide to using the CFPB Financial Well-Being Scale*. Retrieved from http://www.consumerfinance. gov/data-research/research-reports/financial-well-being-scale/

Danes, S. M., & Haberman, H. (2007). Teen financial knowledge, self-efficacy, and behavior: A gendered view. *Journal of Financial Counseling and Planning, 18*(2), 48–60.

De Meza, D., Irlenbusch, B., & Reyniers, D. (2008). *Financial capability: A behavioural economics perspective*. London, UK: Financial Services Authority.

Fernandes, D., Lynch, J. G., Jr., & Netemeyer, R. G. (2014). Financial literacy, financial education, and downstream financial behaviors. *Management Science, 60*(8), 1861–1883. doi:10.1287/mnsc.2013.1849

Financial Consumer Agency of Canada. (2016). *National Strategy for Financial Literacy: Count me in, Canada*. Retrieved from http://www.fcac-acfc.gc.ca/Eng/financialLiteracy/ financialLiteracyCanada/strategy/Documents/NationalStrategyForFinancialLiteracy CountMeInCanada.pdf

Financial Empowerment Champions Project. (n.d.). Retrieved from http://prospercanada.org/ Our-Work/Centre-for-Financial-Literacy/Financial-Empowerment-Champions-Project. aspx

Gjertson, L. (2015). Liquid savings patterns and credit usage among the poor. In J. M. Collins (Ed.), *A fragile balance: Emergency savings and liquid resources for low-income consumers* (pp. 17–37). New York, NY: Palgrave Macmillan.

Hilgert, M. A., Hogarth, J. M., & Beverly, S. (2003). Household financial management: The connection between knowledge and behavior. *Federal Reserve Bulletin, 89*, 309.

Huang, J., Nam, Y., Sherraden, M., & Clancy, M. (2015). Financial capability and asset accumulation for children's education: Evidence from an experiment of child development accounts. *Journal of Consumer Affairs, 49*(1), 127–155. doi:10.1111/joca.2015.49.issue-1

Huang, J., Nam, Y., & Sherraden, M. S. (2013). Financial knowledge and Child Development Account policy: A test of financial capability. *Journal of Consumer Affairs, 47*(1), 1–26.

Hurst, E., & Ziliak, J. P. (2006). Do welfare asset limits affect household saving? Evidence from welfare reform. *Journal of Human Resources, 41*(1), 46–71. doi:10.3368/jhr.XLI.1.46

Jamison, J. C., Karlan, D., & Zinman, J. (2014). *Financial education and access to savings accounts: Complements or substitutes? Evidence from Ugandan youth clubs* (Working Paper No. 20135). National Bureau of Economic Research. Retrieved from http://www.nber.org/ papers/w20135

Johnson, E., & Sherraden, M. S. (2007). From financial literacy to financial capability among youth. *Journal of Sociology and Social Welfare, 34*, 119.

Kempson, E., & Collard, S. (2006). *Financial capability baseline survey: Questionnaire*. Financial Services Authority. Retrieved from http://www.bristol.ac.uk/media-library/sites/ geography/migrated/documents/pfrc0604.pdf

Kempson, E., Collard, S., & Moore, N. (2005). *Measuring financial capability: An exploratory study (No. 37)*. London, United Kingdom: Financial Services Authority. Retrieved from http://www.bristol.ac.uk/media-library/sites/geography/migrated/documents/pfrc0510.pdf

Lewis, M., & Elliott, W. (2014). *Lessons to learn: Canadian insights for U.S. children's savings account (CSA) policy*. Lawrence, KS: Assets and Education Initiative, University of Kansas.

Loke, V., Choi, L., & Libby, M. (2015). Increasing youth financial capability: An evaluation of the MyPath savings initiative. *Journal of Consumer Affairs, 49*(1), 97–126. doi:10.1111/joca.2015.49.issue-1

Lusardi, A., & Mitchell, O. S. (2014). The economic importance of financial literacy: Theory and evidence. *Journal of Economic Literature, 52*(1), 5–44. doi:10.1257/jel.52.1.5

Muthén, B., Toit, S. H. D., & Spisic, D. (1997). Robust inference using weighted least squares and quadratic estimating equations in latent variable modeling with categorical and continuous outcomes. *Psychometrika, 75*, 1–45.

National Council of Welfare. (2010). *Welfare Incomes 2009 (No. 129)*. Ottawa, ON: National Council on Welfare.

Prosper Canada. (2016). *Financial Empowerment Champions Project*. Retrieved October 16, 2016, from http://prospercanada.org/Our-Work/Centre-for-Financial-Literacy/Financial-Empowerment-Champions-Project.aspx

Rice, L., & Bansak, C. (2014). The effect of welfare asset rules on auto ownership, employment, and welfare participation: A longitudinal analysis. *Contemporary Economic Policy, 32*(2), 306–333. doi:10.1111/coep.2014.32.issue-2

Robb, C. A., & Woodyard, A. S. (2011). Financial knowledge and best practice behavior. *Journal of Financial Counseling and Planning, 22*(1), 60–70.

Ross, L., & Nisbett, R. (1991). The person and the situation: Perspectives of social psychology. In *McGraw-Hill series in social psychology*. New York, NY: McGraw-Hill.

Sen, A. (1999). *Development as freedom*. New York, NY: Knopf.

Sherraden, M. (1991). *Assets and the poor: A new American welfare policy*. Armonk, NY: M.E. Sharpe.

Sherraden, M. S. (2013). Building blocks of financial capability. In J. Birkenmaier, M. S. Sherraden, & J. Curley (Eds.), *Financial education and capability: Research, education, policy, and practice* (pp. 3–43). New York, NY: Oxford University Press.

Sherraden, M. S., Huang, J., Frey, J. J., Birkenmaier, J., Callahan, C., Clancy, M., & Sherraden, M. (2015). *Financial capability and asset building for all (No. 13)*. Baltimore, MD: American Academy of Social Work and Social Welfare.

Statistics Canada. (2009). *Canadian Financial Capability Survey (CFCS)*. Retrieved from http://www23.statcan.gc.ca/imdb/p2SV.pl?Function=getSurvey&SDDS=5159

Sullivan, J. X. (2006). Welfare reform, saving, and vehicle ownership do asset limits and vehicle exemptions matter? *Journal of Human Resources, 41*(1), 72–105. doi:10.3368/jhr.XLI.1.72

Taylor, M. (2011). Measuring financial capability and its determinants using survey data. *Social Indicators Research, 102*(2), 297–314. doi:10.1007/s11205-010-9681-9

Xiao, J. J., Chen, C., & Chen, F. (2014). Consumer financial capability and financial satisfaction. *Social Indicators Research, 118*(1), 415–432. doi:10.1007/s11205-013-0414-8

Appendix

Objective financial knowledge scale		
	unweighted correct responses	
Question and responses	n	%
1. If the inflation rate is 5% and the interest rate you get on your savings is 3%, will your savings have at least as much buying power in a year's time? Yes **No** Don't know	9577	65.6
2. A credit report is...? A list of your financial assets and liabilities A monthly credit card statement **A loan and bill payment history** A credit line with a financial institution Don't know	6183	42.4
3. Who insures your stocks in the stock market? The National Deposit Insurance Corporation The Securities and Exchange Commission The Bank of Canada **No one** Don't know	5108	32.9
4. By using unit pricing at the grocery store, you can easily compare the cost of any brand and any package size. **True** False Don't know	10643	68.6
5. If each of the following persons had the same amount of take home pay, who would need the greatest amount of life insurance? **A young single woman with two young children** A young single woman without children An elderly retired man, with a wife who is also retired A young married man without children Don't know	11496	74.1
6. If you had a savings account at a bank, which of the following statements would be correct concerning the interest that you would earn on this account? Sales tax may be charged on the interest that you earn You cannot earn interest until you pass your 18th birthday **Earnings from savings account interest may not be taxed** **Income tax may be charged on the interest if your income is high enough** Don't know	10735	69.2
7. Inflation can cause difficulty in many ways. Which group would have the greatest problem during periods of high inflation that lasts several years? Young working couples with no children Young working couples with children Older, working couples saving for retirement **Older people living on fixed retirement income** Don't know	8027	51.7
8. Lindsay has saved $12,000 for her university expenses by working part-time. Her plan is to start university next year and she needs all of the money she saved. Which of the following is the safest place for her university money? Corporate bonds Mutual Funds	9280	59.8

(Continued)

(Continued).

Objective financial knowledge scale

Question and responses	unweighted correct responses	
	n	%
A bank savings account		
Locked in a safe at home		
Stocks		
Don't know		
9. Which of the following types of investment would best protect the purchasing power savings in the event of a sudden increase in inflation?	5476	35.3
A twenty-five year corporate bond		
A house financed with a fixed-rate mortgage		
A 10-year bond issued by a corporation		
A certificate of deposit at a bank		
Don't know		
10. Under which of the following circumstances would it be financially beneficial to borrow money to buy something now and repay it with future income?	3506	22.6
When something goes on sale		
When the interest on the loan is greater than the interest obtained from a savings account		
When buying something on credit allows someone to get a much better paying job		
It is always beneficial to borrow money to buy something now and repay it with future income		
Don't know		
11. Which of the following statements is not correct about most ATM (Automated Teller Machine) cards?	10241	65.9
You can get cash anywhere in the world with no fee		
You must have a bank account to have an ATM		
You can generally get cash 24 hours-a-day		
You can generally obtain information concerning your bank balance at an ATM machine		
Don't know		
12. Which of the following can hurt your credit rating?	12945	83.4
Making late payments on loans and debts		
Staying in one job too long		
Living in the same location too long		
Using your credit card frequently for purchases		
Don't know		
13. What can affect the amount of interest that you would pay on a loan?	10129	65.3
Your credit rating		
How much you borrow		
How long you take to repay the loan		
All of the above		
Don't know		
14. Which of the following will help lower the cost of a house?	12677	81.7
Paying off the mortgage over a long period of time		
Agreeing to pay the current rate of interest on the mortgage for as many years as possible		
Making a larger down payment at the time of purchase		
Making a smaller down payment at the time of purchase		

*Note. Correct answers are bolded.

Financial self-efficacy scale (unweighted)		
Question and responses	Mean	SD
1. How would you rate your level of financial knowledge?	2.65	.83
Very knowledgeable		
Knowledgeable		
Fairly knowledgeable		
Not very knowledgeable		
How would you rate yourself on each of the following areas of financial management...?[†]		
2. Keeping track of money	3.00	.91
3. Making ends meet*	3.23	.84
4. Shop around to get the best financial product such as loans or insurance rates	2.81	1.01
5. Staying informed on financial issues	2.46	.97

Note. [†] Responses ranged from Very good (4), Good (3), Fairly good (2), Not very good (1). *Dropped from the scale after exploratory factor analysis.

Promoting Financial Capability of Incarcerated Women for Community Reentry: A Call to Social Workers

Cynthia K. Sanders

ABSTRACT

Female incarceration rates are increasing at unprecedented rates. The majority of women are poor single mothers, serving sentences for nonviolent drug-related and property offenses. Among challenges faced when transitioning back into society are a history of interpersonal violence and financial instability. This study examines literature with regard to the barriers women experience with an emphasis on financial struggles and explores outcomes of one initiative to begin addressing the financial capability of women in a minimum security prison. Findings reveal women benefited from the class experience. Social workers are called upon for additional financial capability programming and research in this area.

Female incarceration rates are increasing at an unprecedented rate. In recent decades, the increase in the female prison population has continuously surpassed that of the male prison population, making women the fastest growing segment of the US prison population (Allen, Flaherty, & Ely, 2010; p. 160; Greene, Pranis, & Frost, 2006; Mallicoat, 2012; Section X, p. 491). Between 1980 and 2010, the number of women in prison increased by 646%. There are over 200,000 incarcerated women constituting nearly 10% of the total U.S. prison and jail population. Additionally, there are over one million women on probation or parole (American Civil Liberties Union, 2009; The Sentencing Project, 2012).

"Women in prison are among the most vulnerable and marginalized members of society" (Women in Prison Project, 2006, p. 4). The majority of women involved in the criminal justice system are poor single mothers, most of whom are serving sentences for nonviolent drug-related and property offenses (Mallicoat, 2012; Moe & Ferraro, 2006; Section X, p. 492). Black women imprisonment rates are nearly three times that of White non-Hispanic women (Guerino, Harrison, & Sabol, 2012). The erosion of social service benefits in the welfare state alongside the passage of draconian laws against drug use has resulted in America's war on drugs sometimes being referred to as a war on poor and minority women (Bush-Baskette, 2000; Van Wormer, 2008). Over 95% of state prisoners will be released at some point back into society (Hughes & Wilson, 2015). Although gender-responsive programing has received more attention in recent years, practices in correctional settings are still largely developed for and by men, and women are often an afterthought in terms of incarceration planning and planning for reentry (Mallicoat, 2012; pp 1–12; Thompson, 2010). Gender-responsive approaches for women could focus on a variety of issues, including the fact that women are more likely than men to be the custodians of their children (Allen et al., 2010), and high documented rates of domestic violence among incarcerated women (Zust, 2008). Although this article focuses on a gender-specific initiative as it pertains to domestic violence, financial education, and empowerment, this article does not intend to diminish the need for gender-responsive programs and prison reform for men as well.

Women face many challenges when transitioning back into society. The magnitude of policy and institutional change that is needed to address these challenges is beyond the scope of this article. However, one key challenge women face when reentering communities is financial stability (O'Brien & Lee, 2006). Financial issues are frequently reported as a major concern among inmates and frequently a factor in why women offend in the first place (Johnson, 2014). In the context of multiple oppressions, women's financial knowledge and access to financial resources is severely limited. Additionally, given the alarming rates of a history of domestic violence, women may find themselves isolated from financial information and resources, and prone to economic reliance on an abusive partner (Sanders, 2014a; Zust, 2008). Promoting financial capability that involves both financial knowledge and access to financial resources (Birkenmaier, Sherraden, & Curley, 2013) may provide one tool for increasing women's economic stability upon reentry by improving women's ability to recognize economic abuse, independently manage finances, learn skills to cope with financial problems, and differentiate between reputable financial services and predatory lenders (Postmus, Plummer, McMahon, & Zurlo, 2012; Sanders, 2013). Financial management skills are essential in daily life, from running a household to making ends meet. In addition, providing financial education skills are associated with psychosocial well-being including, economic empowerment and financial self-efficacy among women (Postmus et al., 2012; Sanders, Weaver, & Schnabel, 2007). Advancing women's financial literacy may be especially important because, in general, women consistently demonstrate lower financial literacy than men (Bucher-Koenen, Lusardi, Alessie, & Van Rooij, 2016). In this study, the term *financial literacy* refers to skills and knowledge that allow individuals to make informed and effective decisions given their financial resources. It also includes a dimension of financial empowerment and financial self-efficacy that reflects a person's sense of hope and confidence in meeting financial goals (Weaver, Sanders, Schnabel, & Campbell, 2009). The key distinction between financial literacy and financial capability is that to be financially capable, people must be more than financially literate, they must also have access to financial products and services (Birkenmaier et al., 2013). Financial literacy might be viewed as a step toward building financial capability, but not sufficient to do so.

This study examines current literature with regard to the barriers women experience when reentering society following incarceration, with an emphasis on economic struggles. Additionally, this study examines the outcomes of a financial education and empowerment program developed with the needs of woman survivors of intimate partner violence (IPV) in mind that was delivered in a minimum security women's correctional facility (n = 288).

Review of the literature

Barriers to reentry

"Women inmates represent a myriad of voices that speak to poverty-stricken lives, histories of abuse, separations of mothers and children, struggles with substance abuse, problematic family relationships, health issues, and economic hardships" (Johnson, 2014, p. 365). Among the most difficult barriers women face in the reentry process are economic in nature including limited education, social capital, or marketable skills (Travis & Stacey, 2010). Additionally, access to social welfare programs, to which women may initially turn for economic support, are restricted due to drug-related crimes (Allard, 2002; Johnson, 2014). For example, unless they opt out, all states deny federal benefits such as Supplemental Nutrition Assistance Program (SNAP) and Temporary Assistance for Needy Families (TANF) to people convicted in state or federal courts of felony drug offenses. The ban is imposed for no other offenses but drug crimes (Mauer & McCalmont, 2013). Social and human capital deficiencies, along with the all-too-often disenfranchised community context to which women return, paints a picture in which the odds seem stacked against women for successful reintegration.

Literature consistently documents the difficult histories of incarcerated women (Allen et al., 2010). Themes that continuously emerge include poverty, abuse, mental health problems, and victimization. Prior to incarceration, women are more likely to live in poverty, less likely to have been employed, and more likely to have lower educational levels and lower household incomes than their incarcerated male counterparts (Mallicoat, 2012; Section X, p. 493; Moe & Ferraro, 2006). These factors, among others, present significant barriers to successful community rentry and are factors in recidivism among women (Alleyne, 2006). According to an analysis of recidivism data from 15 states, 58% of women released from state prison in

1994 were rearrested, 38% were reconvicted, and 30% returned to prison within 3 years (Deschenes, Owen, & Crow, 2007, p. 22). It is noteworthy that more current statistics on recidivism rates by gender are not available.

History of violence

Incarcerated women are at higher risk of various forms of violence historically and may continue to experience physical, psychological, or sexual abuse while they are incarcerated (Kim, 2003). One of the most widely prevalent characteristics among incarcerated women is the extremely high rate of historical physical and sexual abuse—as much as 80%—and at least 50% of female inmates report having been abused by intimate partners (Harrison & Beck, 2006). Additionally, a history of exchanging sex for drugs or money for many incarcerated women demonstrates how female inmates may lose control over their lives through domestic violence, street violence, and disempowering life circumstances (Sherman, German, Cheng, Marks, & Baily-Kloche, 2006). Finally, it is important to acknowledge the role of economic abuse in domestic violence. Evidence indicates that abusive partners often engage in economic abuse and use a variety of tactics that negatively impact women financially (Postmus, Plummer, McMahon, Murshid, & Kim, 2012; Sanders, 2014a). Based on in-depth qualitative interviews with women survivors, Sanders (2014a) reported that among other things, abusive partners may completely control household financial resources, monitor spending, use money for sexual exploitation, leave women's names off of bank accounts, and intentionally cause credit problems. This may leave women isolated from financial information and "unbanked" (Whitehouse.gov, 2016). To meet their basic needs, as well as those of children, women may become economically dependent on abusive partners. Additionally, abusive partners often engage in behaviors that restrict a woman's ability to pursue education, or gain and maintain employment that might result in greater financial autonomy (Sanders, 2014a).

Research also demonstrates that even while incarcerated, women may continue to experience abuse from intimate partners. Women may continue to be controlled, manipulated, threatened, and even stalked by their abusers. Examples of tactics include refusing to bring children for visits thus maintaining isolation; interfering with access to legal assistance; and threatening family members (Richie, 2001). Thus, women often experience abuse prior to incarceration, continue to be vulnerable to abuse while incarcerated, and frequently return to abusive relationships and high-risk environments following incarceration.

Financial capability initiatives and research are lacking with women in prison who may be survivors of domestic violence. However, research on financial literacy and capability initiatives with survivors of domestic violence outside of the prison context have reported positive and promising outcomes. For example, a controlled study that examined the Allstate Foundation financial education curriculum, by Postmus, Hetling, and Hoge (2015) reported treatment group outcomes of greater financial knowledge, financial intentions and behaviors, and a decrease in financial strain.

A financial capability initiative using the Redevelopment Opportunities for Women's Economic Action Program (REAP) curriculum paired with an individual development account (matched savings) program provided women an opportunity to apply financial knowledge to savings behavior and access to a bank account. Among 125 women, approximately two-thirds reached their savings goal and 76% made a least one matched savings withdrawal. On average, women saved $1,045 and received a two-to-one match resulting in average savings accumulation of $3,041. Matched withdrawals were used to facilitate asset development including post-secondary education, small business development, or purchase of a reliable vehicle. Additionally, a few unique accounts were used for safety planning; which may, for example, enable a woman to move to a different state, or secure independent housing (Sanders, 2014b).

Economic barriers and financial literacy

Among the most cited economic barriers for women transitioning back into society are employment; safe, decent, and affordable housing; reliable transportation; monthly fees such as monthly parole supervision fees or restitution; and an inability to pay basic monthly expenses such as rent, utilities, food, clothing, health care, and child care costs (Johnson, 2014; O'Brien, 2001; O'Brien & Lee, 2006). According to a study by Johnson (2014), the immediate financial goal among women on parole was to have a job with enough salary to pay basic needs and a limited amount of money for unexpected situations. Although correctional facilities may provide reintegration programing on a variety of topics including life skills, jobs skills, parenting skills, substance abuse treatment, coping skills, and others, one area that appears lacking is in financial literacy (Poby, 2009). Additionally, gender-specific and gender-sensitive programs are lacking. Using male programming may reinforce power inequalities and gender stereotypes (Bloom, Owen, & Covington, 2005). The United States Department of Justice National Institute of Corrections recognizes that women have unique and diverse sets of risks and needs based on lived experiences that should be addressed through women centered programing (Bloom, Owen, & Covington, 2005).

> Gender-responsive means creating an environment through site selection, staff selection, program development, content, and material that reflects an understanding of the realities of women's lives and addresses the issues of the participants. Gender-responsive approaches are multidimensional and are based on theoretical perspectives that acknowledge women's pathways into the criminal justice system. These approaches address social (e.g., poverty, race, class, and

gender inequality) and cultural factors, as well as therapeutic interventions. These interventions address issues such as abuse, violence, family relationships, substance abuse, and co-occurring disorders. They provide a strength-based approach to treatment and skill building. The emphasis is on self-efficacy. (Bloom, Owen, & Covington, 2005, p. 2)

Financial knowledge and skills are important daily living tools that may help support household and family financial stability, and in some cases may even help prevent criminal behavior. Because many of the crimes women commit are money related (drug offenses, property violations, prostitution etc.) finding ways to empower women economically and increase their financial capability may help reduce risk of recidivism and improve economic well-being. Providing financial literacy programing to incarcerated women is an opportunity to reach a very vulnerable population that may otherwise be missed through other systems (Alemagno & Dickie, 2005).

Research on financial literacy with prison populations is very limited to date. Two studies (Call, 2011; Koenig, 2007) have examined the level of financial literacy among male inmates. Poby (2009) developed a financial education program for incarcerated women but does not appear to have tested the effects. Additional initiatives may be under way, such as teaching the FDIC Money Smart Program in prison (ourprisonneighbors.org). However, this initiative appears to be gender neutral and thus does not take into account unique circumstances women may face including domestic violence.

This study examines whether or not the provision of a financial education curriculum designed with the unique needs of women survivors in mind results in increased financial literacy. Implications include the need to move beyond financial literacy to advancing the financial capability of women reentering communities following incarceration.

Methodology

Participants

Women who are part of this study (*N* = 288) were incarcerated at the South Boise Women's Correctional Center (SBWCC) and participated in the Treasure Valley Economic Action Program (TVEAP). They voluntarily participated in the TVEAP program between July, 2012 and October, 2014. SBCC is a transition and treatment facility for minimum-security female offenders. SBWCC provides various rider programs, including the Correctional Alternative Placement Program (CAPP), Traditional Rider, and Therapeutic Community. Additionally, residents may be at SBWCC in the work opportunity program, be probation violators who have returned to serve a term, or be *termers* who have been sentenced to a term of incarceration of over 1 year (https://www.idoc.idaho.gov/content/prisons).

Rider programs are a sort of middle ground between going to prison and being placed on felony probation. Essentially, a defendant is given a prison sentence but placed in a rider program instead. If the defendant successfully completes the program within 365 days, he or she may be placed on probation, rather than completing a prison term. The CAPP rider program includes a 90-day substance abuse treatment program, traditional rider program is focused on cognitive and behavioral change and is generally 5–6 months; and a Therapeutic Community Rider is more intensive and typically lasts between 9–12 months and also typically involves substance abuse treatment (http://atkinsonlawoffices.com/blog/rider/). Almost half of the women in this study (49%, $n = 140$) were in the CAPP or therapeutic community rider program (a limitation of the data is there is no distinction between women in one or the other); 35% ($n = 100$) were in a traditional rider program; 9% ($n = 25$) were in the work center; 8% ($n = 22$) were termers and one participant was serving a term due to probation violation.

TVEAP is a community-based economic education initiative aimed toward survivors of IPV and takes place the Boise, Idaho region. The curriculum is delivered in several locations throughout the treasure valley by instructors employed through the Women and Children's Alliance, a domestic violence service provider whose vision is "to foster a community where individuals thrive in safe, healthy relationships" (http://www.wcaboise.org). The Women and Children's Alliance was approached by the Idaho Department of Corrections and asked to deliver the curriculum within the SBWCC, indicating their understanding that many of their residents had histories of intimate partner violence.

TVEAP utilizes the REAP 12-hr financial education and credit counseling program (Redevelopment Opportunities for Women [ROW], 2005; Sanders et al., 2007). The REAP curriculum is a financial education program developed with the unique needs of women survivors in mind (Sanders et al., 2007) and underscores safety issues as a central component; including discussion of economic abuse in intimate partner relationships, short- and long-term financial goals, and focuses on not only strategies that address basic financial skills, but also approaches that empower women and give them a sense of hope about their financial future (Sanders & Schnabel, 2006). As warranted, the instructors adjusted the curriculum to be relevant to the circumstances of women currently incarcerated with an emphasis on the applicability of content as women transition back into society. Although women were incarcerated, they voluntarily participated in the TVEAP classes.

REAP curriculum

The REAP curriculum was developed through a collaborative of 13 domestic violence service agencies and three homeless agencies in the St. Louis,

Missouri region (Sanders & Schnabel, 2006). The curriculum is made up of four courses that build on each other, although each class can also stand alone. To begin, each woman is given an economic action plan (EAP) they will work on over the course of four class sessions. The EAP guides women as they create financial goals and learn to view themselves as competent financial actors. Safety is an important part of the curriculum, which recognizes that safety considerations may force women to deviate from financial goals when IPV is present. For the incarcerated women in this study, these concepts are placed in the context of their previous life experiences as well as thinking about how safety and healthy relationships are important as they transition back into society.

Section one emphasizes economic empowerment. Women explore their feelings about money and begin to examine the factors that have shaped their financial situation. Many women who have experienced IPV and economic abuse have had limited opportunities to discuss their feelings about money, or the role that financial matters may have played in experiences of IPV (Sanders, 2014a; Weaver et al., 2009) . Section two helps women develop a budget (cost of living plan) that would meet their more immediate needs, as well as enabling them to begin to think about ways to accomplish long-term economic goals. The importance of organizing financial and personal documents, learning about budgets and financial terms, and identifying "spending leaks" are emphasized (Redevelopment Opportunities for Women, 2006). Safety considerations include acknowledging that women may be limited to making only small financial decisions and goals, especially at first, because they may lack control over household expenses and spending.

Section three focuses on understanding credit and debt. Women learn about their credit report. They are given specific steps that will help improve their credit and achieve personal goals. Examples of safety considerations include making sure a credit report can be mailed to a safe address and whether an abuser can access her credit report (using a social security number) and learn where she is living. In such cases, the class facilitator brainstorms with participants how they might go about getting their credit report safely.

Section four examines financial products and services, savings, and investments, as well as potentially predatory alternative financial services. Although bank accounts may be financially optimal for many women, some women are not comfortable opening a bank account for a variety of reasons, such as safety, credit history, or discrimination. Additionally, for women with criminal records gaining access to financial institutional structures may be even more complicated. Safety considerations may include opening new financial accounts at a financial institution other than that of an abusive partner, and using an employment address or post office box for financial mailings.

As a whole, the REAP curriculum promotes women's empowerment and financial self-determination, provides hands-on skills, and aims to increase knowledge of and access to financial resources, increase women's self-confidence in managing and coping with financial issues, and assist women in identifying feasible short- and long-term financial goals through an individualized EAP. REAP was designed with the needs of survivors of IPV in mind (which a large proportion of incarcerated women are) but not with the needs of incarcerated women specifically in mind. Thus, as noted early, instructors adjust the curriculum as they deem relevant to the circumstances of women currently incarcerated with an emphasis on the applicability of content as women transition back into society. Nonetheless, this is also a limitation of the program. However, providing women with tools to take positive financial steps upon community reentry is viewed as positive measure.

Data

Data for this study were acquired by the researcher as secondary data from the Women and Children's Alliance with identifying information removed. Data were entered into SPSS for data analysis. Participants of TVEAP were asked by course instructors to complete a series of forms, including pre/post quizzes for each of the four classes offered, and a written informed consent. Course instructors explained the program and informed women that by filling out the forms they were agreeing to allow use of the data for program evaluation and research purposes.

Instruments

Several data collection instruments are routinely used by the Women and Children's Alliance in delivery of the TVEAP program. These include a participant enrollment and consent to participate form, a demographic information survey, an economic abuse checklist, and pre and post quizzes for each of the four modules of the 12-hr economic education curriculum.

I developed the economic abuse checklist at the request of the Women and Children's Alliance when TVEAP was initiated in the Boise, Idaho region. They utilize this checklist in their intake process with shelter clients and collect this information at all of their TVEAP classes. Their purpose is to document the degree to which their target population experiences the economic abuse dimension of IPV. I developed the checklist based on research about economic abuse and tactics of abusive partners (Adams, Sullivan, Bybee, & Greeson, 2008; Weaver et al., 2009). It includes 20 item indicators of the presence or absence of economic abuse. Women answer each question in nominal terms of yes or no as it relates to their most recent relationship.

For each of the four classes, a simple quiz is used to assess whether or not participants are acquiring basic knowledge. The four quizzes were created collaboratively with staff from the Women and Children's Alliance when they began to deliver the curriculum in the Boise, Idaho area. They are designed to assess basic content in each of the four class areas including economic empowerment, credit and debt, budgets and costs of living, and financial products and services. Questions are true/false, multiple choice, and fill in the blank in nature. Questions assess both factual knowledge about financial planning and credit repair (e.g., A credit card is an example of what type of credit? Name the three credit bureaus. True or false: A safety deposit box is the best place to keep the only copy of your will?) as well as understanding and attitudinal outcomes related to economic abuse and empowerment (e.g., Name the four types of abuse. Increasing your ability to make positive choices about your own destiny' is the definition of?). Based on the number of questions, quiz one is worth 10 points, quiz two 7 points, quiz three 7 points, and quiz four 5 points. Taken together, a combined score for all four classes could range from 0–29 points. Methods for acquiring, analyzing, and reporting data for this study were approved through a university institutional review board.

Data analysis

Data were analyzed using SPSS. Descriptive analyses are conducted to examine the characteristics of 288 incarcerated women who voluntarily participated in the TVEAP program between July, 2012 and October, 2014; economic abuse checklist to monitor whether and to what extent women have experienced economic abuse in their most recent intimate relationship; and pre and post quiz scores for each of the four classes as well as total combined score. Paired sample t-tests were used to examine whether pre and post quiz scores change significantly. Analysis of variance was used to examine whether outcomes differed by program status (traditional rider, therapeutic community, etc.). Not all 288 women completed all four sections and/or both pre and post quizzes. Thus, data is shown for those who completed both pre and post measures for each quiz and for those who completed pre/post measures for all four classes combined. This ranged from all 287 women completing pre and post measures on quiz number one to only 270 women completing all four pre/post measures for analysis of total combined score outcomes (see Table 3).

Findings

Women's characteristics

Table 1 provides basic demographic information about the women in this study. Women ranged in age from 20 to 62 with an average age of 34 years. The majority of women were White (78%). Although this is consistent with a

Table 1. Women's demographic characteristics (N = 288).

Characteristic	
Race	
White	225 (78%)
Latina/Hispanic	24 (8%)
Bi-Racial	22 (8%)
American Indian	10 (4%)
Black/non-hispanic	3 (1%)
Asian/Pacific Islander	2 (1%)
Other	2 (1%)
Education	
Less than High School	35 (12%)
High School or GED	118 (41%)
Some College	74 (26%)
2-Year Degree	17 (6%)
4-Year Degree	4 (2%)
Attended Graduate School	2 (1%)
Missing	38 (13%)
Age (Mean)	34 (median 31, range 20–62)
Children	
Average number	2 (median 2, range 0–8)
Children 18 or under	210 (73%)
Yes	78 (27%)
No	

majority Caucasian population of Idaho, it is not congruent with the over-representation of Hispanics and African Americans in Idaho prisons. Based on 2006 census data, the Hispanic population in Idaho was 9.1%; the Hispanic prison population was 15.8%. Additionally, the African American population in Idaho was 0.6%, and the African American prison population in Idaho was 2.1% (http://www.safetyandjustice.org/node/1537/). This difference could imply that either Hispanic and African American women chose not to participate in the TVEAP program, or they may have been less likely to be residents of the minimum security program.

Generally, women had minimal education with over half of women (53%) with a high school degree or less and less than 10% of women had completed a two-year degree or more. Almost three-quarters of women had children age 18 or younger.

Economic abuse

To examine the extent to which economic abuse was relevant to lives of women participating in the TVEAP program while incarcerated, they completed an economic abuse checklist that included 20 questions about economic abuse indicating whether or not a woman's most recent partner engaged in such tactics (Table 2). The number of indicators women reported experiencing ranged from zero (n = 20, 7%) to 18 with an average of 10. All but 20 women reported experiencing at least one indicator of economic abuse. Fifty percent of women reported experiencing between nine and 10

Table 2. Economic abuse checklist indicators in most recent relationship (N = 288).

Indicator	Yes %	No %
Does your partner prevent you from working or attending school?	50%	50%
Does your partner interfere with work performance through harassing and monitoring your activities?	51%	32% 17% NA
Does your partner make you feel as though you don't have a right to know any details about money or household resources?	55%	45%
Does your partner prevent you from having access to household money or financial resources?	62%	38%
Does your partner steal money from you or your family?	50%	50%
Does your partner force you to give access to your accounts?	39%	61%
Does your partner refuse to help support the family financially?	46%	54%
Does your partner destroy your personal belongings?	74%	26%
Does your partner make financial or investment decisions that affect you or your family without consulting you?	71%	29%
Does your partner overuse your credit cards or refuse to pay the bills (negatively impacting your credit)?	58%	42%
Does your partner prevent you from owning or using credit cards or bankcards?	34%	66%
Does your partner refuse to put your name on bank accounts?	63%	37%
Does your partner refuse to put your name on other financial assets (such as a home)?	35%	65%
Does your partner forbid you from having a bank account?	17%	83%
Does your partner use money to force you to have sex?	19%	81%
Does your partner demand you hand over your paychecks?	34%	51% 15% NA
Does your partner make you account for every penny you spend?	54%	46%
Does your partner require you to provide receipts for all your purchases (for example when you go to the grocery store)?	43%	57%
Does your partner withhold physical resources including food, clothes, necessary medications, or shelter for you and/or our children?	26%	74%
Does your partner take your car keys to prevent you from using the car?	65%	35%

indicators. These data demonstrate that the majority of women had experienced some degree of economic abuse in their most recent relationship suggesting the REAP curriculum which emphasizes safety and financial matters as they relate to survivors of IPV is highly relevant.

Financial literacy

TVEAP offers four financial education classes based on the REAP curriculum. Data were gathered from 288 women although not all women completed pre and post-tests for all four courses. Table 3 presents pre and post quiz scores for each of the four sections, as well as total score and change scores among women completing all four classes. A series of paired sample *t*-tests were performed to assess whether post-test scores were significantly higher than pre-test scores. Quizzes one through four, as well as total scores, were tested. Significant improvement in the number of questions answered correctly occurred in quiz one ($t = -27.54$, $p < .001$); quiz 2 ($t = -15.65$, $p \leq .001$); quiz 3 ($t = -28.34$, $p \leq .001$); quiz 4 ($t = -25.95$, $p \leq .001$); and total

Table 3. Pre and post quiz scores.

Quiz 1 10 Points Possible	Questions Correct		Percent Correct	
Pretest score	(N = 288, Missing = 0)	Mean = 5.96 Median = 6	Range = 0 to 10	Mean = 59.6% Median = 60%	Range = 0% to 100%
Posttest score*	(N = 287, Missing = 1)	Mean = 8.79 Median = 9	Range = 2 to 10	Mean = 87.9% Median = 90%	Range = 20% to 100%
Change in # or %	(N = 287, Missing = 1)	Mean change = 2.79 Median = 3	Range = −2 to 9	Mean change = 27.9% Median = 30%	Range = −20% to 90%
287 women completed pre and post quiz; 264 out of 287 improved (92%)				
Quiz 2 7 Points Possible	**Questions Correct**		**Percent Correct**	
Pretest score	(N = 282, Missing = 6)	Mean = 5.23 Median = 6	Range = 0 to 7	Mean = 74.7% Median = 86%	Range = 0% to 100%
Posttest score*	(N = 283, Missing = 5)	Mean = 6.47 Median = 7	Range = 2 to 7	Mean = 92.5% Median = 100%	Range = 29% to 100%
Change in # or %	(N = 282, Missing = 6)	Mean change = 1.25 Median = 1	Range = −1 to 7	Mean change = 18.2% Median = 14%	Range = −14% to 100%
282 women completed pre and post quiz; 194 out of 232 improved (69%)				
Quiz 3 7 Points Possible	**Questions Correct**		**Percent Correct**	
Pretest score	(N = 277, Missing = 11)	Mean = 3.45 Median = 3	Range = 0 to 7	Mean = 49.3% Median = 43%	Range = 0% to 100%
Posttest score*	(N = 277, Missing = 11)	Mean = 6.49 Median = 7	Range = 2 to 7	Mean = 92.8% Median = 100%	Range = 29% to 100%
Change in # or %	(N = 277, Missing = 11)	Mean change = 3.05 Median = 3	Range = −1 to 7	Mean change = 43.5% Median = 43%	Range = −14% to 100%
277 women completed pre and post quiz; 250 out of 277 improved (90%)				
Quiz 4 5 Points Possible	**Questions Correct**		**Percent Correct**	
Pretest score	(N = 272, Missing = 16)	Mean = 2.74 Median = 3	Range = 0 to 5	Mean = 54.9% Median = 60%	Range = 0% to 100%

(Continued)

Table 3. (Continued).

Quiz 1 10 Points Possible	Questions Correct		Percent Correct	
Posttest score*	(N = 272, Missing = 16)	Mean = 4.55 Median = 5	Range = 0 to 5	Mean = 91% Median = 100%	Range = 0% to 100%
Change in # or %	(N = 272, Missing = 16)	Mean change = 1.82 Median = 2	Range = −2 to 5	Mean change = 36.1% Median = 40%	Range = −40% to 100%

272 women completed pre and post quiz; 242 out of 272 improved (89%)

Combined 29 Points Possible	**Questions Correct**		**Percent Correct**	
Pretest score	(N = 270, Missing = 18)	Mean = 17.35 Median = 17	Range = 3 to 27	Mean = 60% Median = 59%	Range = 10% to 93%
Posttest score*	(N = 270, Missing = 18)	Mean = 26.29 Median = 27	Range = 13 to 29	Mean = 90.7% Median = 93%	Range = 45% to 100%
Change in # or %	(N = 270, Missing = 18)	Mean = 8.92 Median = 9	Range = 0 to 19	Mean change = 30.4% Median = 31%	Range = 0% to 66%

270 women completed ALL 8 quizzes; 269 out of 270 improved (99.6%)

*posttest score significantly higher than pretest score $p \leq .05$

score ($t = -43.21$, $p \leq .001$). Additionally, all pre/post test scores were examined in subgroups based on program status (excluding the one participant who was serving a term due to cell size) using analysis of variance (ANOVA). No significant differences between groups were found based on F-scores and p-values all greater than .05.

Among women completing all four pre/posttest measures ($N = 270$), the average pretest score averaged 17 and improved to 26 points at posttest. This represents a nine point gain or 30% improvement on average. All t-tests were statistically significant ($p \leq .001$) providing evidence that on average women made significant gains in their financial knowledge.

Discussion

Findings from this study demonstrate that the TVEAP is serving survivors of domestic violence who are economically disadvantaged, experience economic abuse, and show significant increases in their financial literacy following completion of the REAP curriculum. Findings reveal that women benefit from the class experience and information provided but call for additional financial capability programing with incarcerated women who will transition back into society and evaluation measures. That is, although women had positive financial literacy outcomes, promoting financial capability will also require greater efforts to connect women to financial resources, services, and asset building initiatives as they reenter society to act on what they have learned and make progress in financial stability.

Importantly, TVEAP advances financial capability efforts through the provision of classes that are empowerment based and designed with the circumstances of women and safety issues as the central component. The results are promising, but limited. This is an exploratory and descriptive study that examined the extent to which incarcerated women would increase their financial literacy through participation in an economic education class. It is worth mentioning that anecdotally the instructors of these courses have noted that the women who are incarcerated are, in their estimation, the most engaged (compared to other locations where they also teach classes) and overtly grateful for the opportunity to participate in discussions around financial struggles, economic abuse, and planning for the future economic well-being for themselves and their children.

Although women acquired skills and knowledge to help them make healthy financial choices postincarceration, women continue to face challenges within the broader social and institutional contexts of life once released. This frequently includes poverty and survival in disenfranchised neighborhoods. Women are simultaneously attempting to identify housing; obtain a job; reestablish social relationships, which may include domestic violence; frequently attempting to regain custody of children; maintain sobriety; and adhere to conditions of probation or parole.

Unfortunately, most women released from jail or prison likely return to the same disenfranchised neighborhoods, difficult conditions, and inadequate services and resources to assist women in the reentry process. Women continue to be challenged by unemployment, inadequate affordable housing options, health and mental health care needs, and the need for safety from trauma and abuse (Richie, 2001). Additionally, given the high prevalence of drug-related crimes for which women are incarcerated in this country, long-term substance abuse treatment and prevention are a necessity to maintain abstinence postincarceration (Richie & Johnsen, 1996). With more adequate resources in place, women will be better positioned to use the knowledge and skills learned in an economic education program as a meaningful tool.

Neighborhood development efforts are also needed so that when women are released, they find communities more equipped to provide the support they need. That is, the economic conditions in their neighborhoods need to change for them to successfully reengage with community life. Greater financial capability efforts are needed once women leave prison for them to safely apply the knowledge and skills they gain from programs such as the one presented here (Sanders, 2013; Sanders, 2014b). Financial capability moves beyond financial literacy and allows people to "to understand, access, and act in their best financial interest" (Johnson & Sherraden, 2007, p. 124). Financial capability requires financial literacy, but also requires access to appropriate financial products. In other words, financial capability requires both the *ability to act* (knowledge, skills, confidence, and motivation) and the *opportunity to act* (through access to beneficial financial products and institutions; Johnson & Sherraden, 2007, p. 136). For example, building bridges with financial institutions for women to begin establishing a credit record may support them in their efforts to acquire stable housing, and reliable transportation.

Feelings of hopelessness are reported to frequently characterize the experiences of women arrested in the United States (Chapman, Specht, & Cellucci, 2005; Richie, 2001). Thus, providing women with meaningful tools is essential. The TVEAP initiative is one that aims to promote a sense of hope, orientation toward the future, and accomplishment of short-term goals and identification of longer-term goals. However, for these tools to take hold, structural and community barriers to economic success must also be addressed. Successful reintegration can only become a reality when women are connected to effective reentry programs that provide assistance with employment, housing, child care, transportation and basic economic needs (Johnson, 2014, p. 385).

Women also need access to antipoverty resources such as cash assistance and food stamps as a temporary source of support. Thus, policy provisions that deny access to social welfare programs to women convicted of felony drug-related acts serve only to potentially increase the chances that women will be driven back to crime related activities to survive (Allard, 2002). Having access to basic economic needs first is likely to position women who participate in economic education and financial capability initiatives such as TVEAP to be even more effective in making financial decisions and managing resources in order to maintain economic stability for themselves and children.

Limitations and research implications

This study is exploratory and descriptive in nature, and thus only begins to scratch the surface of understanding the benefits of financial literacy programs with incarcerated women. The study is limited to a pre-/posttest design, with no further follow-up. A 3-month follow-up and follow-up with participants following release from the SBWCC to examine the applicability of course content upon reentry would have strengthened the current study. The secondary data source is based on a convenience sample of women who voluntarily participated in the TVEAP program. Thus, the study cannot be generalized beyond the sample and no control group was used to assess outcomes with and without the intervention. Finally, the sample is homogeneous in nature and does not reflect the overrepresentation of Hispanics and African American in the Idaho prison system.

Further studies are needed, including controlled studies and qualitative studies. Qualitative inquiry would help shed light on understanding how a curriculum designed with the needs of survivors in mind could be made even more applicable to the needs of incarcerated women as they transition back into communities. Additionally, studies which examine the benefits, such as economic stability and domestic violence/healthy relationships, that may be associated with increased financial literacy once women transition back into their communities are critical. Going beyond financial literacy to issues of financial capability and understanding access to institutional structures that allow women to act on what they have learned will also be important (e.g., affordable banking services, ability to build a credit record, financial autonomy, etc.).

The measures used in this study are also simplistic in capturing financial literacy. The quizzes given before and after each class are very simple in nature and measure only the most basic financial knowledge. That is, they are not comprehensive in measuring all of the content of classes. It is also conceivable that administration of quizzes to participants by course instructors could bias outcome scores. However, measuring the content more comprehensively was prohibitive in this study as it would require significant time from participants to fill out a measure and thus take away from valuable class time.

A call to social works

Studies suggest that supportive services, such as education, substance abuse and mental health treatment, counseling, and rehabilitation programing, are not routinely available to women in prison. When they do exist they are often not gender-sensitive (Mallicoat, 2012; Richie, 2001). Although social workers are not as prevalent in the correctional field as they could be (Agllias, 2004), the relevance of society's interaction with women coming out of prison—who in turn struggle with poverty, homelessness, child custody, substance abuse, domestic violence, HIV and other health and mental health conditions—is clear (O'Brien & Young, 2006).

Given the vulnerable status of women in prison and the intersection of correctional issues with poverty, racism, and others, it is critical that the social work profession make efforts to have greater visibility. Recent trends in social work practice and education emphasize the importance of financial capability work (Birkenmaier et al., 2013). Providing economic empowerment and financial capability programs that contribute to household stability and security are vital. To do this, however, social workers must be more adequately prepared to conduct effective financial assessments with clients struggling with complex financial problems and economic circumstances, and integrate financial issues into social work (Gillen & Loeffler, 2012; Loke, Watts, & Kakoti, 2013). Curriculum content in social work education needs to be integrated into courses on practice, policy, theory, research, and applied in practicum settings for social workers to become competent in delivering financial capability interventions at micro, mezzo, and macro levels.

Empowerment-based approaches to working with vulnerable women align well with a social work orientation (Turner & Maschi, 2015). Empowerment and consciousness raising approaches suggest that an important influence on a person's ability to make individual change is the extent to which she has an understanding of multiple influences on her behavior (Freire, 1970; Richie, 2001). For incarcerated women, strategies to help them develop critical insight into structural influences on personal choices, rather than self-blame or simply focusing on self-esteem, may be especially relevant (Richie, 2001). Providing financial education and importantly promoting greater financial capability structures at an institutional level may enable women to make financial decisions that provide greater options for economic success. Social workers grounded in community and social development models are well positioned to initiate and promote structural change.

Conclusion

Despite the odds being stacked against them, some women do manage to successfully negotiate the transition from prison to community (O'Brien, 2001). One should not underestimate their strengths and capacities while simultaneously advocating for programmatic resources and structural and policy change. Research indicates that women coming out of prison require both individualistic responses to their situations and addressing the ongoing economic and social constraints they face (Johnson, 2014; O'Brien & Young, 2006; Richie, 2001). This study makes a contribution by demonstrating that women in prison are receptive and in need of efforts to advance their financial capability. Social workers are called upon to engage in initiatives to advance the financial capability of incarcerated women as they transition back into families, neighborhoods, and communities.

References

Adams, A. E., Sullivan, C. M., Bybee, D., & Greeson, M. R. (2008). Development of the scale of economic abuse. *Violence Against Women, 14*(5), 563–588. doi:10.1177/1077801208315529

Agllias, K. (2004). Women in corrections: A call to social work. *Australian Social Work, 57,* 331–342. doi:10.1111/asw.2004.57.issue-4

Alemagno, S., & Dickie, J. (2005). Employment issues of women in jail. *Journal of Employment Counseling, 42,* 67–74. doi:10.1002/joec.2005.42.issue-2

Allard, P. (2002). *Life sentences: Denying welfare benefits to women convicted of drug offenses.* Washington, DC: Sentencing Project.

Allen, S., Flaherty, C., & Ely, G. (2010). Throwaway moms: Maternal Incarceration and the criminalization of female poverty. *Affilia: Journal of Women and Social Work, 25*(2), 160–172. doi:10.1177/0886109910364345

Alleyne, V. (2006). Locked up means locked out: Women, addiction and incarceration. *Women and Therapy, 29,* 181–194. doi:10.1300/J015v29n03_10

American Civil Liberties Union. (2009). *Women and the criminal justice system.* Retrieved from https://www.aclu.org/prisoners-rights/women-prison

Birkenmaier, J. M., Sherraden, M., & Curley, J. C. (Eds.). (2013). *Financial capability and asset development: Research, education, policy, and practice.* New York, NY: Oxford University Press.

Bloom, B., Owen, B., & Covington, S. (2005). *Gender-responsive strategies for women offenders: A summary of research, practice, and guiding principles for women offenders.* Washington, DC: National Institute of Corrections, U.S. Department of Justice. Retrieved from http://static.nicic.gov/Library/020418.pdf

Bucher-Koenen, T., Lusardi, A., Alessie, M., & van Rooij, M.C.J. (2016). How financially literate are women? An overview and new insights. (WP 2016–1). *Global Financial Literacy Excellence Center (GFLEC).* Washington, DC: The George Washington University. Retrieved from http://gflec.org/wp-content/uploads/2016/02/WP-2016-1-How-Financially-Literate-Are-Women.pdf

Bush-Baskette, S. (2000). The war on drugs and the incarceration of mothers. *Journal of Drug Issues, 30,* 919–928. doi:10.1177/002204260003000414

Call, L. L. (2011). *Exploring financial knowledge, behaviors, and economic socialization in an incarcerated population: A mixed methods analysis* (Theses and Dissertations). Paper 2641.

Chapman, A. L., Specht, M. W., & Cellucci, T. (2005). Factors associated with suicide attempts in female inmates: The hegemony of hopelessness. *Suicide and Life-Threatening Behavior, 35*(5), 558–569. doi:10.1521/suli.2005.35.5.558

Deschenes, E. P., Owen, B., & Crow, J. (2007). *Recidivism among female prisoners: Secondary analysis of the 1994 BJS Recidivism Data Set.* Washington, DC: U.S. Department of Justice. Retrieved from www.ncjrs.gov/pdffiles1/nij/grants/216950.pdf

Freire, P. (1970). *Pedagogy of the oppressed.* New York, NY: Continuum.

Gillen, M., & Loeffler, D. N. (2012). Financial literacy and social work students: Knowledge is power. *Journal of Financial Therapy, 3*(2), 28–38. doi:10.4148/jft.v3i2.1692

Greene, J., Pranis, K., & Frost, N. (2006). *The Punitiveness Report—Hard Hit: The growth in imprisonment of women, 1977–2004.* New York, NY: Institute on Women and Criminal Justice, Women's Prison Association. Ebook.

Guerino, P., Harrison, P. M., & Sabol, W. J. (2012). *Prisoners in 2010.* Washington, DC: U.S. Department of Justice Office of Justice Programs, Bureau of Justice Statistics.

Harrison, P., & Beck, A. (2006). *Prisoners in 2005*. Bureau of Justice Statistics Bulletin, NCJ 215092. Retrieved from http://www.bjs.gov/content/pub/pdf/p05.pdf

Hughes, R., & Wilson, D. J. (2015). *Reentry trends in the United States: Inmates returning to the community after serving time in prison*. Washington, DC: Bureau of Justice Statistics. Retrieved from www.bjs.gov/content/reentry/reentry.cfm

Johnson, E., & Sherraden, M. S. (2007). From financial literacy to financial capability among youth. *Journal of Sociology and Social Welfare*, *34*(3), 119–145.

Johnson, I. M. (2014). Economic impediments to women's success on parole: "We need someone on our side.". *The Prison Journal*, *94*(3), 365–387. doi:10.1177/0032885514537760

Kim, S. (2003). Incarcerated women in life context. *Women's Studies International Forum*, *26*(1), 95–100. doi:10.1016/S0277-5395(02)00358-8

Koenig, L. A. (2007). Financial literacy curriculum: The effect on offender money management skills. *Journal of Correctional Education*, *58*(1), 43–56.

Loke, V., Watts, J. L., & Kakoti, S. A. (2013). Financial capabilities of service providers in the asset building field. In J. M. Birkenmaier, M. Sherraden, & J. C. Curley (Eds.), *Financial capability and asset development: Research, education, policy, and practice*. New York, NY: Oxford University Press.

Mallicoat, S. L. (2012). Women and crime: A text/reader, Section I. In S. L. Mallicoat & C. Estrada Ireland (Eds.), *Women and crime: An introduction*. Thousand Oaks, CA: Sage.

Mauer, M., & McCalmont, V. (2013). *A lifetime of punishment: The impact of the felony drug ban on welfare benefits*. The Sentencing Project: Research and Advocacy for Reform. Retrieved from http://sentencingproject.org/wp-content/uploads/2015/12/A-Lifetime-of-Punishment.pdf

Moe, A. M., & Ferraro, K. J. (2006). Criminalized mothers: The value and devaluation of parenthood behind bars. *Women and Therapy*, *29*, 135–164. doi:10.1300/J015v29n03_08

O'Brien, P. (2001). Just like baking a cake: Women describe the necessary ingredients for successful reentry after incarceration. *Families in Society: The Journal of Contemporary Human Services*, *82*(3), 287–297. doi:10.1606/1044-3894.200

O'Brien, P., & Lee, N. (2006). Moving from needs to self-efficacy: A holistic system for women in transition from prison. *Women and Therapy*, *29*(3/4), 261–284. 24. doi:10.1300/J015v29n03_14

O'Brien, P., & Young, D. S. (2006). Challenges for formerly incarcerated women: A holistic approach to assessment. *Families in Society: The Journal of Contemporary Social Services*, *87*(3), 359–366. doi:10.1606/1044-3894.3540

Poby, K. E. (2009). *Women's financial future: A financial literacy program for incarcerated women* (Dissertation). Chicago School of Professional Psychology

Postmus, J. L., Hetling, A., & Hoge, G. L. (2015). Evaluating a financial education curriculum as an intervention to improve financial behaviors and financial well-being of survivors of domestic violence: Results from a longitudinal randomized controlled study. *Journal of Consumer Affairs*, *49*(1) 250–266. doi:10.111/joca.12057

Postmus, J. L., Plummer, S. B., McMahon, S., Murshid, N. S., & Kim, M. S. (2012). Understanding economic abuse in the lives of survivors. *Journal of Interpersonal Violence*, *27*(3), 411–430. doi:10.1177/0886260511421669

Postmus, J. L., Plummer, S. B., McMahon, S., & Zurlo, K. A. (2012). Financial literacy: Building economic empowerment with survivors of violence. *Journal of Family Economic Issues*, *34*, 275–284. doi:10.1007/s10834-012-9330-3

Redevelopment Opportunities for Women (ROW). (2005). *Realizing Your Economic Action Plan (REAP)* (Published curriculum). St. Louis, MO: Author.

Redevelopment Opportunities for Women (2006). *Realizing Your Economic Action Plan (REAP)* Curriculum. St. Louis, MO: Author.

Richie, B. E. (2001). Challenges incarcerated women face as they return to the communities: Findings from life history interviews. *Crime & Delinquency, 47*, 368–389. doi:10.1177/0011128701047003005

Richie, B. E., & Johnsen, C. (1996). Abuse histories among newly incarcerated women in a New York City jail. *Journal of the American Medical Women's Association, 51*, 111–114.

Sanders, C. K. (2013). Financial capability among survivors of domestic violence. In J. M. Birkenmaier, M. Sherraden, & J. C. Curley (Eds.), *Financial capability and asset development: Research, education, policy, and practice.* New York, NY: Oxford University Press.

Sanders, C. K. (2014a). Economic abuse in the lives of women abused by an intimate partner: A qualitative study. *Violence Against Women*, 1–27. doi:10.1177/1077801214564167

Sanders, C. K. (2014b). Savings for survivors: An individual development account program for survivors of intimate partner violence. *Journal of Social Service Research, 40*(3), 297–312. doi:10.1080/01488376.2014.893950

Sanders, C. K., & Schnabel, M. (2006). Organizing for economic empowerment of battered women: Women's savings accounts. *Journal of Community Practice, 14*(3), 47–68. doi:10.1300/J125v14n03_04

Sanders, C. K., Weaver, T. L., & Schnabel, M. (2007). Economic education for battered women: An evaluation of outcomes. *Affilia: Journal of Women and Social Work, 22*(3), 240–254. doi:10.1177/0886109907302261

Sherman, S. G., German, D., Cheng, Y., Marks, M., & Baily-Kloche, M. (2006). The evaluation of the JEWEL project: An innovative economic enhancement and HIV prevention intervention study targeting drug using women involved in prostitution. *AIDS Care, 18*(1), 1–11. doi:10.1080/09540120500101625

The Sentencing Project: Research and Advocacy for Reform. (2012). *Fact sheet: Incarcerated women.* Retrieved from http://www.sentencingproject.org/doc/publications/cc_Incarcerated_Women_Factsheet_Dec2012final.pdf

Thompson, A. (2010). *Releasing prisoners, redeeming communities: Reentry, race, and politics.* New York, NY: NYU Press.

Travis, L., & Stacey, J. (2010). A half century of parole rules: Conditions of parole in the United States, 2008. *Journal of Criminal Justice, 38*, 604–608. doi:10.1016/j.jcrimjus.2010.04.032

Turner, S. G., & Maschi, T. M. (2015). Feminist and empowerment theory and social work practice. *Journal of Social Work Practice, 29*(2), 151–162. doi:10.1080/02650533.2014.941282

Van Wormer, K. (2008). Anti-feminist backlash and violence against women worldwide. *Social Work and Society, International Online Journal, 6*(2) 324–337,

Weaver, T. L., Sanders, C. K., Schnabel, M., & Campbell, C. L. (2009). Development and preliminary psychometric evaluation of the domestic violence-related financial issues scale. *Journal of Interpersonal Violence, 24*(4), 569–585. doi:10.1177/0886260508317176

Whitehouse.gov. (2016). *Financial Inclusion in the United States.* Council of Economic Advisers Brief. Washington, DC. Retrieved from https://www.whitehouse.gov/sites/default/files/docs/20160610_financial_inclusion_cea_issue_brief.pdf

Women in Prison Project of the Correctional Association of New York. (2006). *When "free" means losing your mother: The collision of child welfare and the incarceration of women in New York State.* Retrieved from http://www.correctionalassociation.org/wp-content/uploads/2012/05/When_Free_Rpt_Feb_2006.pdf

Zust, B. L. (2008). Assessing and addressing domestic violence experienced by incarcerated women. *Creative Nursing, 14*(2), 70–72. doi:10.1891/1078-4535.14.2.70

Toward Culturally Sensitive Financial Education Interventions with Latinos

Liza Barros Lane and Suzanne Pritzker

ABSTACT

To expand the financial capability of Latinos, culturally sensitive interventions are needed. A literature search was conducted to examine how financial education interventions have been used to improve financial outcomes for Latinos. Just 7 peer-reviewed intervention studies were identified, suggesting a substantial gap in knowledge in this area. Although conclusions about the effectiveness of financial education interventions with Latinos are limited, each study finds positive changes in financial attitudes or behaviors. Using Resnicow's (1999) cultural sensitivity framework, surface and deep structure methods of tailoring financial education were identified. Implications for designing and testing culturally sensitive financial education interventions are discussed.

Financial education has been theorized as an antidote for financial challenges. Through teaching budgeting and financial management, financial education is believed to increase financial success for those who struggle with achieving financial well-being. However, empirical findings regarding the effectiveness of financial education interventions are mixed (Van Rooij, Lusardi, & Alessie, 2011). The financial challenges faced by the rapidly growing Latino population in the United States signal a need for greater understanding of how financial education interventions impact Latinos and ways in which these interventions could be strengthened to meet the needs of this population. This article reviews and synthesizes the existing literature on financial education with Latinos in order to inform culturally sensitive financial practice and research with Latino families and communities.

Literature review

The financial well-being of latinos

By 2060, Latinos will represent 29% of the US population (Colby & Ortman, 2015). Although sharing cultural similarities and a common language,

Latinos are a heterogeneous population, incorporating recent immigrants from across Latin America, as well as multigenerational US citizens. Across these distinct national backgrounds and citizenship statuses, Latinos in the United States struggle to achieve financial security. Financial inclusion, defined as having access to financial institutions with appropriate and safe products and services (Sherraden, 2013), is low among Latinos. Only 56% of Latino immigrants have bank accounts (Perry, 2008), and comparatively few have access to pension plans (Santos & Seitz, 2000). Low financial inclusion has made Latino immigrants more susceptible to such challenges as predatory lending (Center for Responsible Lending, 2004), a lower likelihood of qualifying for loans toward asset building, e.g., home ownership (Harrington, 2004), and a higher likelihood of being forced to borrow at much higher interest rates when they do receive loans (Datta, 2011). Latino retirement savings substantially lag behind other ethnic groups even when controlling for access to retirement plans, income, age, and job descriptions (Ariel/Aon Hewitt, 2012). If their financial situation remains as it is now, over 90% of Latino seniors will not have enough funds to support them through the end of their lives (Meschede, Shapiro, Sullivan, & Wheary, 2010).

Latino financial attitudes and values

Cultural factors may influence how Latinos approach financial matters. The value of *familismo* prioritizes family loyalty and cohesion, incorporating expectations of allegiance to and responsibility for family members beyond the nuclear family (Comeau, 2012). This value can be seen in the practice of sending remittances (money) to loved ones in their country of origin even before paying for their bills (Suro, Bendixen, Lowell, & Benavides, 2002). *Familismo* declines as acculturation increases (Steidel & Contreras, 2003), suggesting that more assimilated Latinos are less likely to feel responsible for extended family's financial well-being. Another example of a cultural value that may impact Latinos' financial behaviors is *personalismo*, valuing personal relationships over distantly formal relationships. Latinos are more likely to seek advice from a relative or friend and less likely to do so from a financial professional (De Rubio, 2013).

Structural barriers to financial stability

Structural barriers may contribute to the financial insecurity many Latinos experience. Such obstacles, which may be particularly challenging for immigrant Latinos, must be understood to inform culturally sensitive adaptations to financial education interventions.

Documentation status

Those lacking documentation face barriers to accessing mainstream financial services and assets such as insurance and homes (Meraz, Petersen, Marczak, Brown, & Rajasekar, 2013). For example, although banks increasingly accept Mexican *matriculas* or identification from other countries (Suro et al., 2002), they often do not approve mortgage or car loans for undocumented immigrants.

Undocumented immigrants are often unable to obtain stable and safe employment. They may look for employment off the books, resulting in worker exploitation without labor protections (Heyman, 1998) and limited access to health benefits or retirement plans (Santos & Seitz, 2000), making affordable healthcare and safe retirement unattainable.

Location of banks and predatory lending services. The lack of proximity and access to banks in predominantly Hispanic neighborhoods is a barrier to Latino participation in financial institutions. Even where banks are present, Latino residents may find check cashing and other predatory financial businesses more accessible based on location and hours of service (Bair, 2005). Predatory lenders have targeted lower income Latino and African American neighborhoods, offering subprime mortgages with high and variable interest rates and leaving residents vulnerable to home foreclosures when interest rates balloon (Barwick, 2010).

Mistrust of the banking industry. Latinos report high levels of fear and distrust in financial institutions leading to low utilization of banks and disconnect with the mainstream financial system in the United States (Bair, 2005; Fisher & Hsu, 2012). This may be attributable in part to instability in Latin American banking systems in the 1980s and 1990s (Perry, 2008).

Language

An estimated 37.6 million people speak Spanish at home (González-Barrera & López, 2013). Even when controlling for education and income, this has been correlated with disconnect from financial institutions in the United States (Perry, 2008). Likewise, greater use of English is positively linked with bank usage among Latinos.

Toward culturally sensitive financial education interventions

Financial capability theory suggests that financial behavior is influenced by both an individual's financial knowledge and skills and environmental characteristics such as institutional access to appropriate financial products (Sherraden, 2013). Given the cultural values and financially-oriented structural barriers Latinos experience, culturally sensitive adaptations to financial education may be needed (Soehl & Waldinger, 2010). To inform the design of such interventions, it is important to examine frameworks for culturally sensitive adaptations. A key source of such frameworks comes from health care scholarship. Culturally sensitive interventions in health care increase patient satisfaction with, and access to, healthcare, with the end result of decreasing health disparities among diverse groups in the United States (Anderson, Scrimshaw, Fullilove, Fielding, & Normand, 2003). Though limited research examines disparities in financial education between Latinos and other ethnic groups, a similar rationale can guide culturally sensitive adaptations of financial education interventions to reduce gaps in financial well-being between Latinos and non-Hispanic Whites.

There is some consensus that culture is "learned, shared, and transmitted from one generation to the next, and it can be seen in a group's values, norms, practices, systems of meaning, ways of life, and other social regularities" (Kreuter, Lukwago, Bucholtz, Clark, & Sanders-Thompson, 2003, p. 133). Values and norms that may impact financial behaviors have been transmitted across generations of Latinos. Yet, not every Latino/a upholds these values equally, as factors such as acculturation, generational status, immigrant status, and years in the United States may impact how these values are manifest (Kreuter et al., 2003).

A leading framework (Resnicow, Baranowski, Ahluwalia, & Braithwaite, 1999) for culturally sensitive intervention adaptations suggests that cultural sensitivity is two-pronged, addressing surface structure and deep structure. Surface structure adaptations maintain the original intervention content while manipulating materials to match characteristics of the targeted ethnic group (e.g., altering pictures of people and places, language use, references to music and food, etc.). Deep structure adaptations acknowledge differences in core cultural values, reflect on how these may influence behaviors, and intentionally incorporate these differences into intervention content (Resnicow et al., 1999).

To examine how financial education interventions can improve financial outcomes, this study examines all existing English-language peer-reviewed literature studying financial education with Latinos. Specifically, this study (a) systematically examines the current state of knowledge of financial education interventions relative to Latinos, (b) describes the cultural adaptations to financial education interventions based on Resnicow and colleagues' (1999) cultural sensitivity model, and (c) identifies a culturally sensitive agenda for advancing research in this area.

Methods

Search strategy

A literature search was conducted to identify all peer-reviewed articles and any gray literature examining financial education interventions with Latino/

as. Ten scholarly databases were searched: Academic Search Complete, Business Source Complete, Chicano Database, EconLit, Education Source, Humanities Full Text (H. W. Wilson), Social Work Abstracts, SocINDEX with Full Text, Family Studies Abstracts, and PsycINFO. Social Services Abstracts was not searched as that database was not accessible to us. The following search terms were used: "financial education" OR "financial capability" OR "financial literacy" OR "personal finance" OR "family finance," paired with AND (Latino* OR Hispanic*). The search was limited to English language peer-reviewed articles, with no date parameters. The gray literature utilized the same search terms and was limited to trade publications, working papers, and dissertations. A more limited Google Scholar search was conducted using just the terms "financial education" AND Hispanic* or Latino* as those terms had yielded the most relevant results in the prior searches.

Study inclusion and exclusion criteria

The following inclusion criteria were established: (a) studies assessing the outcomes of financial education interventions; (b) samples in which the majority (over 50%) were Latinos living in the United States or outcome data was collected on a Latino subsample; and (c) empirical studies, using qualitative, quantitative, or mixed research methods.

Screening and assessment

Our search of scholarly databases yielded 53 articles; after exact duplicates were removed, 33 remained. Of these, six were selected based on their titles and abstracts. Two were removed after reviewing article content because they did not specifically assess financial education outcomes. The gray literature search generated 87 papers, none of them meeting the inclusion criteria of reporting outcomes of a financial education intervention with a Latino sample or subsample. The Google Scholar search yielded 1,290 articles; after reviewing all titles and abstracts, three more scholarly articles were selected. When there was some question as to whether the inclusion criteria had been met, we discussed each article together until an agreement was reached. This was the case for an article in which the Latino composition of the pretest sample was clearly delineated, but not of its posttest sample (Zhan, Anderson, & Scott, 2006). We discussed the article and agreed to include it because there was no indication in the article that the composition of the posttest sample differed significantly from the pretest sample.

In total, these search processes yielded seven articles. As a validity check, each article's reference list, as well as related documents and articles that cited any of these seven articles, were reviewed in search of other relevant articles examining financial education interventions with Latinos. This process yielded no additional articles.

Analysis procedures

We originally intended to assess these articles using the 27-item PRISMA systematic review checklist (Moher, Liberati, Tetzlaff, & Altman, 2009). However, because only one randomized control trial was identified and a number of the identified studies were qualitative in nature, traditional systematic review tools were not applicable. Instead, we identified five aspects of the PRISMA checklist applicable to this analysis: study characteristics (e.g, methodology, sample size, and study duration), characteristics of study participants, study quality, intervention model, and study findings regarding financial knowledge, attitudes, and behaviors. Using a leading cultural sensitivity framework (Resnicow et al., 1999), we also analyzed the use of surface and deep structural adaptations in each financial education intervention.

Results

Study characteristics

Of the seven identified studies, three used qualitative methods, and four used quantitative methods. Three used quasi-experimental designs while one used a randomized control trial. The sample size among these studies ranged from six to 300, as indicated in Table 1. In two of the quantitative studies, the timing of the posttest was not reported (Spader, Ratcliffe, Montoya, & Skillern, 2009; Zhan, Anderson, & Scott, 2009); one study collected follow-up data at 1 month postintervention (Hetling, Postmus, & Kaltz, 2015), and one collected data at both 1 month and 16 months after the intervention (Zhan et al., 2006). All qualitative studies used posttest designs. Sprow Forte (2012) did not report the timing of the posttest; Meraz et al. (2013) collected data 6 months postintervention and Higginbotham, Tulane, and Skogrand (2012) collected data both after the intervention and 1 year later.

Characteristics of study participants

Three of the seven studies solely studied Latinos (Meraz et al., 2013; Spader et al., 2009; Sprow Forte, 2012). Of the studies that reported participants' gender, women comprised at least 77% of each sample (Hetling et al., 2015; Meraz et al., 2013; Sprow Forte, 2012; Zhan et al., 2006, 2009). Three study samples only included Latino/a immigrants (Meraz et al., 2013; Spader et al., 2009; Zhan et al. 2009), one was limited to blended step families

Table 1. Intervention summary and results.

Study	Intervention	Study Design/ Methods	N	Outcomes	Surface Structure	Deep Structure
Hetling et al. (2015)	Traditional financial education: *Moving Ahead Through Money*	Randomized Control Trial	300 (Latina n = 177)	Significant changes in financial knowledge and behaviors regarding financial planning and savings.	-Spanish language	-Content geared towards financial information for women who need to safely leave an abusive relationship
Spader et al. (2009)	Alternative financial education: 13-episode *Nuestro Barrio* telenovela	quasi-experimental/ quantitative	66	No significant change in financial literacy; progress along stages of change for bank acct usage, home ownership, level of trust towards banks; increased comfort with financial institutions	-Spanish language -Program name, *Nuestro Barrio* -*Telenovela* format for entertainment value -Ethnically matched actors -In-home viewing for those without contact with financial institutions	-Content geared towards Latino immigrants with no prior experience with U.S. financial services
Zhan et al., (2006, 2009)	Traditional financial education: 12 hours *Financial Links for Low-Income People*	quasi-experimental/ quantitative	163 (Latino n = 30) (n = 52) Latino pre-test	Significant changes in knowledge on predatory lending practices; public and work-related benefits; banking practices; savings and investing strategies; and credit use and interest rates	-Spanish Language	-Evaluation geared towards participants with limited experience with financial services

(Continued)

Table 1. (Continued).

Study	Intervention	Study Design/Methods	N	Outcomes	Surface Structure	Deep Structure
Sprow Forte (2012)	Holistic financial education: *Mujeres Fuertes* 2–15 week semesters of once a week classes	case study/ qualitative	6	Increased empowerment; motivation to reach financial goals; increased savings and credit scores, decreased debt	-Spanish language -Program name, *Mujeres Fuertes* -Located in Latino community -Ethnically matched instructors -Provided child care, housing, food assistance -Hands-on instruction	-Emphasizing historical achievements of Latino/as to build pride -Use of *personalismo* by instructors and participants, sharing their own stories -Potlucks, food sharing to foster deep connections
Meraz et al. (2013)	Traditional financial education: 6–9 hour *Dollar Works 2: A Personal Financial Education Program*	Program evaluation/ qualitative	39	Reported behavioral change: opening a bank acct, negotiating for lower loan interest rates; increased comfort negotiating with financial institutions	-Spanish language -Located in Latino community or neutral locations -Ethnically matched instructors -Flexible class schedules -Hands-on instruction	-Additions to the curriculum based on interest of participants (i.e., home-buying/renting and college savings) -Face-to-face interviews
Higginbotham et al. (2012)	Holistic financial education: 6-week *Smart Steps: Embrace the Journey* for stepfamilies	action research/ qualitative	62 (Latino n = 29)	20 of 29 Latinos reported improved financial practices; decreased conflict over finances; increased control over finances	-Spanish language -Hands on instruction	—Classes taught to couples

(Higginbotham et al., 2012), and one focused on survivors of intimate partner violence (IPV; Hetling et al., 2015).

Study quality

Reflective of the nascent stage of financial education research with Latinos, three of the seven reviewed studies do not integrate quantitative methods that enable measurement of change. These studies justify their rationale for using qualitative methodologies. For example, Meraz and colleagues relied on prior research indicating that Likert scales pose challenges for Spanish speaking participants, instead opting for open-ended measures. Both Higginbotham et al. (2012) and Sprow Forte (2012) explained that the qualitative study designs could help researchers understand why participants believe financial education is necessary and factors impacting the financial education learning process. All three studies utilized triangulation, either through team coding (Meraz et al., 2013; Higginbotham et al., 2012) or by using multiple sources of information including participant self-report, instructor observations, and course documents (Sprow Forte, 2012). Additionally, they appear transferrable to broader Latino populations, with interventions that concur with recommendations from experts in the field. The quantitative studies described their analytic methods clearly, in one case, using a rigorous Randomized Control Trial methodology. More information about procedures used for dealing with missing data would strengthen replication (Spader et al., 2009), as would clearly reporting demographics for both pre/post test participants (Zhan et al., 2009). The quantitative studies might also be strengthened by using objective measures for financial behaviors rather than self-report (Hetling et al., 2015).

Intervention models

The models used by the seven interventions under study fall into three categories. Four used a traditional financial education curriculum. One delivered financial education using an alternative approach. The two remaining studies utilized a holistic approach.

Traditional financial education

Four studies used a traditional classroom educational intervention (Hetling et al., 2015; Meraz et al., 2013; Zhan et al., 2006, 2009). The *Dollar Works 2: A Personal Financial Education Program* (DW2) curriculum focused on financial topics such as financial decision-making, money management skills, income and bank account management, credit, and debt, while the *Financial Links for Low-Income People* (FLLIP) emphasized institutional financial services such as predatory lending practices, public and work-related benefits, banking practices, credit use and interest rates, and personal financial strategies (Zhan et al., 2006, 2009). *Moving*

Ahead Through Money was designed specifically for survivors of IPV. As such, curriculum objectives included learning financial vocabulary and knowledge about money and credit, understanding important financial transactions such as filling out loan applications, filing for bankruptcy, and checking credit scores. The final objective was to learn financial information necessary to leave an abusive situation (Hetling et al., 2015). Unlike the other three educational interventions, this program consisted of both group class meetings and at least one individual meeting.

Alternative financial education curriculum

Spader et al. (2009) studied a traditional financial education curriculum with a nontraditional form of delivery in the form of a *telenovela* (soap opera), a form of entertainment popular in Latin America. *Nuestro Barrio* presented material to Latino immigrants in their own homes with the goal of reaching immigrants who otherwise may not seek out this information. It was comprised of 13 episodes using the plotline and characters' dialogue to indirectly teach financial concepts and to introduce the array of financial services offered in the United States. For example, the show presented the story of Javier, a mechanic, who finally agreed to open up a bank account after his cash savings were robbed, thus giving the viewers a lesson regarding the importance of bank account ownership.

Holistic financial education

The remaining studies (Higginbotham et al., 2012; Sprow Forte, 2012) incorporated traditional classroom financial education as one component of a broader holistic and family-based approach. *Smart Steps: Embrace the Journey* (Higginbotham et al., 2012) sought to support development of a step-family system by teaching participants about the roles each member can play, legal issues, communication with children's parents, and financial education. Financial education was seen as an important curricular component as the unique dynamics stepfamilies bring to the allocation of financial resources can lead to relational stress. *Smart Steps* facilitated discussions about each partner's level of comfort around debt, taught intra-family financial negotiation skills, and incorporated experiential exercises such as creating a list of financial expectations and formulating a budget.

The *Mujeres Fuertes* curriculum was a 3-year cohort program for Latina women. This program viewed its participants holistically in the context of their age, culture, education, family circumstances, etc. (Sprow Forte, 2012). Financial education, life skills, career development, and career classes were taught in two 15-week terms for a total of 30 classes. Alongside the financial education curricula, *Mujeres Fuertes* emphasized personal leadership and helped participants manage their lives and finances through assistance with child care, housing, food, and utilities. The underlying program theory linked financial decisions with personal leadership and growth, "We are always trying to make a connection between the finances and the leadership and how it impacts yourself and your pocket" (Sprowe Forte, 2012, p. 224).

Study findings

Financial knowledge
Four of the studies examined changes in financial knowledge. The *Nuestro Barrio* reported no substantial knowledge changes postintervention (Spader et al., 2009); however, both of the studies utilizing the FLLIP curriculum reported significant changes in knowledge in the posttest (Zhan et al., 2006, 2009). All three of the regression models in Hetling et al.'s (2015) study of survivors of IPV resulted in statistically significant increases in financial knowledge with a large effect size of 1.11.

Attitudinal changes
All four quantitative studies identified changes in financial attitudes, including evidence of increased awareness that financial changes needed to be made. This finding emerged particularly in the quasi-experimental study (Spader et al., 2009), which examined bank usage and homeownership applying the transtheoretical change model. Participants were assessed on where they stood on a five-stage continuum regarding bank account usage or preparation for buying a home, from precontemplation (participants are not aware of the need to change or have no intention to change in the next 6 months) to termination (the new behavior is a part of their life and there is not a temptation to deviate). The treatment group showed significantly more progress than the control group along the stages of change.

Increased empowerment emerged across all qualitative studies. Participants reported feeling greater control of their finances (Higginbotham et al., 2012) and more comfortable negotiating with financial institutions for services like lower loan interest rates or buying a home (Meraz et al., 2013). Spader et al. (2009) identified increased comfort with financial institutions through attitudinal measures such as, "I feel welcome in a bank," and, "I would feel comfortable asking a bank employee for financial advice" (p. 68). Likewise, Zhan and colleagues (2009) found that participants were more likely to open bank accounts and less likely to use alternative financial services such as payday loans after receiving the FLLIP intervention.

Changes in financial behavior
Four studies measured participants' perceptions of the intervention's effect on their financial practices, while one also measured objective indicators of change in financial behaviors (See Table 1) (Sprow Forte, 2012). In one study, participants reported that budgeting improved their organization and helped them integrate saving for emergencies into their regular financial habits (Higginbotham et al.,

2012). By the end of the 3-year program, Sprow Forte (2012) found that female participants' savings had increased, debt had decreased, and their credit scores had increased by 19 points on average.

Meraz et al. (2013) identified behavioral changes; some immigrant participants reported opening new accounts at banking institutions as a result of the intervention. However, Meraz and colleagues also identified a barrier to behavioral change for undocumented immigrants. Some undocumented immigrants found that they were unable to apply what they had learned because they could not access financial services without proper identification.

Hetling et al. (2015) examined how participants made and followed a financial plan and saved extra funds. One month postintervention, the measured financial behaviors improved by 18%. An inverse relationship was found between levels of depression and self-reported financial behaviors, signalling an interplay between mental health and financial behavior.

Cultural sensitivity

Surface structure adaptations

Surface structure adaptations emerged in each intervention (See Table 1). All seven integrated Spanish language, with two adopting Spanish-language titles (Spader et al., 2009; Sprow Forte, 2012). This is a common approach to adapting financial education; for example, the FDIC has translated its financial education curricula into Spanish (Ibarra, 2005). Three hired ethnically-matched financial educators and chose intervention locations in Latino communities (Meraz et al., 2013; Spader et al., 2009; Sprow Forte, 2012). One intervention brought financial education directly to Latino immigrants in their own homes through a culturally familiar *telenovela* (Spader et al., 2009), enabling it to reach individuals who otherwise may not have sought out this information.

The selection of content delivery methods also appeared guided by cultural considerations. For example, in four interventions, hands-on approaches to learning were selected (Zhan et al., 2006, 2009), with two citing evidence from educational research showing their effectiveness among Latino learners (Meraz et al., 2013; Spader et al., 2009). In fact, Meraz et al.'s participants reported that the ability to practice solving real-life problems was more beneficial than learning financial facts.

Deep structure adaptations

All seven interventions employed adaptations that can be characterized as deep structure adaptations, although there was no empirical analysis of the impacts of these adaptations on outcomes. The most common adaptation consisted of adjusting the content to meet perceived financial knowledge needs of participants. For example, information about financial services offered in the United States that would be unfamiliar to people born and raised in Latin America was offered by several interventions (Meraz et al., 2013; Spader et al., 2009). Both studies utilizing the FLLIP curriculum specifically measured outcomes related to predatory lending practices and financial institutions' services due to their importance to the low-income participants and immigrants (Zhan et al., 2006, 2009).

Higginbotham et al. (2012) adapted their financial education curriculum to recognize the cultural value of *familismo* by helping couples discuss financial issues and resolve differences. The researchers found that Latinos responded more favorably to this part of the intervention than other participants, and participants' newly acquired negotiation and discussion skills decreased intra-family conflict over finances and helped family members create unified financial goals.

Deep structure adaptations are most pronounced in *Nuestro Barrio*, where the value of *personalismo* is demonstrated through the characters, such as Ricardo the banker, teaching his friends and family about financial products at family events and social gatherings. *Personalismo*, too, is reflected through the use of face-to-face interviews and individual meetings as part of the intervention (Hetling et al., 2015; Meraz et al., 2013), the sharing of personal financial stories on the part of instructors and participants (Sprow Forte, 2012), and the integration of potlucks to foster connections between participants. Cohorts that shared food had lower attrition rates than those that did not (Sprow Forte, 2012).

Discussion

Limitations

Although this study offers the first comprehensive review of financial educa-tion research with Latinos to our knowledge and important insight into the state of the literature, there are limitations. This body of research is at a nascent stage, as indicated by the small number of studies. Though findings suggest improvements in financial behavior, only one study observed beha-vioral changes, rather than relying on self-report (Sprow Forte, 2012). Additionally, several promising surface and deep structure adaptations were identified; preliminary data suggest that these may positively impact the receptivity of Latinos to financial education. Yet, no studies specifically measured the extent to which participants hold traditional cultural values, nor did they incorporate quantitative measures of the effects of their cultural adaptations. Although these limitations are significant, this analysis of the current state of the literature offers key implications for practice and research focused on the financial education of Latinos.

Implications for culturally sensitive financial practice with latinos

All seven studies reviewed here incorporated either surface and/or deep structure strategies to adapt their financial education interventions. Surface strategies were most prevalent, including incorporating Spanish language, hiring Latino recruiters and instructors, bringing education into participants' homes or communities, accommodating work schedules and child care needs, and incorporating Latino-specific personal stories into content delivery. Qualitative findings offer support for some of these adaptations, including the importance of learning financial information in one's own language from instructors to whom participants could relate, and hands-on instruction. Meraz et al.'s (2013) interviews also indicated that the use of Spanish and accessible locations contributed to participants' learning and their satisfaction.

Higginbotham et al. (2012) integrated a deep structure adaptation that supports the value of *familismo*. In including spouses in the intervention, they found that the Latinos responded more favorably than did non-Latino participants. Designing intervention models in which the whole immigrant family learns together and is supported in reaching agreement on new financial goals can reinforce and strengthen wise financial behaviors (Robles, 2014). Although participants' knowledge did not improve in the *Nuestro Barrio* study, they demonstrated attitudinal changes, such as progress along stages of change and greater comfort with banking, a cornerstone for financial well-being in the United States. These findings suggest that home-based interventions, such as the *telenovela* studied by Spader et al. (2009), offer a possible path for facilitating family-based financial education for Latinos disconnected from the financial mainstream. The analyzed studies demonstrate the relevance of both surface *and* deep cultural adaptations to meet Latinos' needs, although more research is needed about the comparative effectiveness of these strategies.

Recognizing the importance of financial inclusion, several interventions specifically target Latino participants' attitudes toward financial institutions, resulting in more favorable views of mainstream financial institutions and less likelihood to use alternative financial services (Meraz et al., 2013; Spader et al., 2009; Zhan et al., 2009). However, none of the interventions included community-level strategies for addressing barriers, such as lack of access to financial institutions among this population. Meraz et al. (2013) reported that although undocumented participants expressed eagerness to practice new skills, lack of documentation left them unable to apply aspects of what they had learned. A partnership with financial institutions established in the community may be better equipped to address these gaps, in conjunction with curricula that discuss and address community-specific structural barriers. For example, agencies can set the groundwork for financial inclusion, by advocating for affordable accounts or increased presence of financial institutions in primarily Latino neighborhoods; curricula can address local financial institutions that accept identification from other countries and provide low-fee or free accounts.

Although this article has focused on integrating cultural adaptations into financial education, adapting interventions to be in line with traditional Latino values may at times conflict with financial education intervention goals (Resnicow et al., 1999). For example, financial education commonly focuses on building credit, to achieve goals such as homeownership and college education. However, the common aversion to debt among Latino immigrants (McMellon & Moore, 2008) may lead Latinos to prefer to avoid attaining credit. Therefore, adapting financial education interventions to explicitly acknowledge these beliefs and incorporate culturally appropriate strategies to address them may be helpful to program participants.

Implications for financial education research

That we could only identify seven financial education interventions with Latino samples is concerning given the prevalence of Latinos in the United States and the financial struggles they face. The number and types of studies prevented us from generalizing about the impacts of financial education on Latinos. This analysis does, however, yield important next steps in advancing this research. Explicit sample descriptions and generalizable subgroup comparisons, with attention to the diversity of the Latino population can help determine whether interventions are differentially effective for distinct subgroups (Resnicow et al., 1999). To understand the impacts of assimilation, researchers must be clear when testing an intervention which generation(s) of Latinos is being targeted, and with an immigrant sample, length of time in the United States.

Critically, measures of knowledge, attitude, and behavioral outcomes must be culturally and empirically valid. Future research should seek to validate outcome measures with samples of Latino participants in order to facilitate comparisons of interventions. Furthermore, to inform culturally-appropriate —and effective—interventions for Latinos, research must build on knowledge gained from qualitative studies, and quantitatively examine and compare the effectiveness of various surface and deep culturally sensitive strategies in terms of their impacts on the financial knowledge, attitudes, and behaviors of Latinos.

Furthermore, future research should also measure how these strategies impact levels of program engagement and attrition. For example, surface structure adaptations can inform effective recruitment strategies. Since Latinos place a high value on reputational networks, offering educational programs within community organizations with existing ties to the Latino community, or utilizing opinion leaders (such as the *promotora* model in health settings) within the community, may increase recruitment. Researchers can then evaluate such engagement strategies to identify effective approaches. Just one study discussed attrition, a possible challenge to financial education interventions with vulnerable populations, finding that a deep structure adaptation (i.e., sharing food) decreased attrition (Sprow Forte, 2012). Future research should present attrition rates and examine ways in which cultural adaptations may impact attrition.

Conclusion

This study explores the state of knowledge regarding the financial education of Latinos in the United States. It offers the first comprehensive examination of intervention research in this area and, for the first time, applies a culturally sensitive framework to this research (Resnicow et al., 1999). Financial education as a Latino-specific intervention is virtually unchartered territory, but it must be explored to design and implement interventions to increase financial capability among this population. Although the conclusions that can be made about the effectiveness of financial education interventions in supporting Latino families are limited, attention should be paid to designing and testing culturally sensitive interventions that address ways in which this community's cultural strengths and structural barriers impact financial behavior and opportunity.

References

Anderson, L. M., Scrimshaw, S. C., Fullilove, M. T., Fielding, J. E., & Normand, J., & Task Force on Community Preventive Services. (2003). Culturally competent healthcare systems: A systematic review. *American Journal of Preventive Medicine, 24*(3), 68–79. doi:10.1016/S0749 3797(02)00657 8

Ariel/Aon Hewitt Study. (2012). *401(k) Plans in living color: A study of 401(k) savings disparities across racial and ethnic groups.* Chicago, IL: Ariel Education Initiative & Aon Hewitt. Retrieved from https://www.arielinvestments.com/images/stories/PDF/ariel-aonhe witt-2012.pdf

Bair, S. (2005). Improving the access of recent Latin American migrants to the U.S. banking system. In D. F. Terry, & S. R. Wilson (Eds.), *Beyond small change: Making migrant remittances count* (pp. 95–132). Washington, DC: Inter-American Development Bank.

Barwick, C. (2010). Patterns of discrimination against Blacks and Hispanics in the U.S. mortgage market. *Journal of Housing and the Built Environment, 25*(1), 117–124. doi:10.1007/s10901-009-9165-x

Center for Responsible Lending. (2004). *Latino homes at risk: Predatory mortgage lending* (Policy brief 14). Retrieved from http://www.responsiblelending.org/mortgage-lending/research-analysis/ib014-Latino_Homes_at_Risk-1004.pdf

Colby, S. L., & Ortman, J. M. (2015). *Projections of the size and composition of the US Population: 2014 to 2060.* Retrieved from https://www.census.gov/content/dam/Census/library/publications/2015/demo/p25-1143.pdf

Comeau, J. A. (2012). Race/Ethnicity and family contact: Toward a behavioral measure of familialism. *Hispanic Journal of Behavioral Sciences, 34*, 251–268. 0739986311435899. doi:10 1177/0739986311435899

Datta, K. (2011). *New migrant communities and financial services*. London, UK: Friends Provident Foundation.

De Rubio, A. R. (2013). Understanding minority households as consumers of financial services. *Family and Consumer Sciences Research Journal*, *42*(2), 150–161. doi:10.1111/fcsr.12049

Fisher, P. J., & Hsu, C. (2012). Differences in household saving between non-Hispanic White and Hispanic households. *Hispanic Journal of Behavioral Sciences*, *34*(1), 137–159. doi:10.1177/0739986311428891

González-Barrera, A., & López, H. (2013). *Spanish is the most spoken non-English language in US homes, even among non-Hispanics*. Pew Research Org, 13. Retrieved from http://www.pewresearch.org/fact-tank/2013/08/13/spanish-is-the-most-spoken-non-english-language-in-u-s-homes-even-among-non-hispanics/

Harrington, J. (2004, January 5). A culture for lending. *St. Petersburg Times*.

Hetling, A., Postmus, J. L., & Kaltz, C. (2015). A randomized controlled trial of a financial literacy curriculum for survivors of intimate partner violence. *Journal of Family and Economic Issues*, 1–14. Advance online publication.

Heyman, J. M. (1998). State effects on labor exploitation: The INS and undocumented immigrants at the Mexico-United States border. *Critique of Anthropology*, *18*(2), 157–180. doi:10.1177/0308275X9801800203

Higginbotham, B. J., Tulane, S., & Skogrand, L. (2012). Stepfamily education and changes in financial practices. *Journal of Family Issues*, *33*(10), 1398–1420. doi:10.1177/0192513X12450000

Ibarra, B. (2005). *Financial counseling: A meaningful strategy for building wealth in the Latino community*. Washington, DC: National Council of La Raza. Retrieved from http://publications.nclr.org/handle/123456789/1366

Kreuter, M. W., Lukwago, S. N., Bucholtz, D. C., Clark, E. M., & Sanders-Thompson, V. (2003). Achieving cultural appropriateness in health promotion programs: Targeted and tailored approaches. *Health Education & Behavior*, *30*(2), 133–146. doi:10.1177/1090198102251021

McMellon, C. A., & Moore, T. M. (2008). *Financial decision-making by undocumented Central American immigrants: An exploratory study*. Proceedings of the Northeast Business & Economics Association, Melville, NY.

Meraz, A. A., Petersen, C. M., Marczak, M. S., Brown, A., & Rajasekar, N. (2013). Understanding the long-term benefits of a Latino financial education literacy education program. *Journal of Extension*, *51*(6), 1–9. Retrieved from http://www.joe.org/joe/2013december/a3.php

Meschede, T., Shapiro, T. M., Sullivan, L., & Wheary, J. (2010). *Living longer on less: Severe financial insecurity among African-American and Latino seniors* (Report #3). Waltham, MA: Institute on Assets and Social Policy. Retrieved from http://iasp.brandeis.edu/pdfs/Author/meschede-tatjana/Severe%20Financial%20Insecurity.pdf

Moher, D., Liberati, A., Tetzlaff, J., & Altman, D. G. (2009). Preferred reporting items for systematic reviews and meta-analyses: The PRISMA statement. *Annals of Internal Medicine*, *151*(4), 264–269. doi:10.7326/0003-4819-151-4-200908180-00135

Perry, V. (2008). Acculturation, microculture and banking: An analysis of Hispanic consumers in the USA. *Journal of Services Marketing*, *22*(6), 423–433. doi:10.1108/08876040810901846

Resnicow, K., Baranowski, T., Ahluwalia, J. S., & Braithwaite, R. L. (1999). Cultural sensitivity in public health: Defined and demystified. *Ethnicity & Disease*, *9*(1), 10–21.

Robles, B. J. (2014). Economic inclusion and financial education in culturally diverse communities: Leveraging cultural capital and whole-family learning. *New Directions for Adult and Continuing Education, 2014*, 57–66. doi:10.1002/ace.v2014.141

Santos, R., & Seitz, P. (2000). Benefits coverage for Latino and Latina workers. In S. M. Perez, & P. Cattan (Eds.), *Moving up the economic ladder: Latino workers and the nation's future prosperity* (pp. 163–185). Washington, DC: National Council of La Raza.

Sherraden, M. S. (2013). Building blocks of financial capability. In J. Birkenmaier, J. Curley, & M. Sherraden (Eds.), *Financial education and capability: Research, education, policy, and practice* (pp. 3–43). New York, NY: Oxford University Press.

Soehl, T., & Waldinger, R. (2010). Making the connection: Latino immigrants and their cross-border ties. *Ethnic and Racial Studies, 33*(9), 1489–1510. doi:10.1080/01419871003624050

Spader, J., Ratcliffe, J., Montoya, J., & Skillern, P. (2009). The bold and the bankable: How the Nuestro Barrio telenovela reaches Latino immigrants with financial education. *The Journal of Consumer Affairs, 43*(1), 56–79. doi:10.1111/j.1745-6606.2008.01127.x

Sprow Forte, K. (2012). Educating for financial literacy: A case study with a sociocultural lens. *Adult Education Quarterly, 63*(3), 215–235. doi:10.1177/0741713612460267

Steidel, A. G. L., & Contreras, J. M. (2003). A new familism scale for use with Latino populations. *Hispanic Journal of Behavioral Sciences, 25*(3), 312–330. doi:10.1177/0739986303256912

Suro, R., Bendixen, S., Lowell, B. L., & Benavides, D. C. (2002). *Billions in motion: Latino immigrants, remittances, and banking*. Washington, DC: The Pew Hispanic Center and the Multilateral Fund.

Van Rooij, M., Lusardi, A., & Alessie, R. (2011). Financial literacy and stock market participation. *Journal of Financial Economics, 101*(2), 449–472. doi:10.1016/j.jfineco.2011.03.006

Zhan, M., Anderson, S. G., & Scott, J. (2006). Financial knowledge of the low-income population: Effects of a financial education program. *Journal Social & Social Welfare, 33*, 53.

Zhan, M., Anderson, S., & Scott, J. (2009). Banking knowledge and attitudes of immigrants: Effects of a financial education program. *Social Development Issues, 31*(3), 15 32.

From Being Unbanked to Becoming Unbanked or Unbankable: Community Experts Describe Financial Practices of Latinos in East Los Angeles

Larissa A. Padua and Joanna K. Doran

ABSTACT

Appropriate use of formal financial institutions facilitates saving and asset building. Yet 20% of the US Latino population is unbanked. In this cross-sectional qualitative study, 34 community experts were interviewed regarding financial practices in the predominantly low-income Latino and immigrant community of East Los Angeles. Thematic analysis of these in-depth, semistructured interviews suggests that immigration status fuels fears regarding banking and ultimately the persistence of unbanked status; limited financial education prompts community members to move from being unbanked to being unbankable. Techniques employed to reverse this cycle appear helpful, but ultimately overwhelmed by the magnitude of community mistrust and misinformation.

The economic crisis of 2008 compounded existing trends toward greater economic insecurity among a substantial number of families. During the crisis, Latino families have lost two-thirds of their asset holdings (Pew Research Center, 2011), as wages continued to stagnate (Brooks, Wiedrich, Sims, & Rice, 2015). At the same time, the proliferation of alternative financial services (AFS), such as check cashing and payday loan businesses, encourages families with depleted asset holdings to acquire unmanageable debt, which further strips their resources (Center for Responsible Lending, 2015).

Being *banked*, defined as owning an account at a federally insured depository institution, can provide families with lower-cost financial services and a financial record that enhances their ability to acquire assets (Federal Deposit Insurance Corporation [FDIC], 2014). Thus, banking serves as one important component in a household's strategy to attain economic stability (Sherraden, 2013). Despite the important role of banking in the accumulation of assets, 1 in 13 households are still unbanked in the United States, and this number increases to nearly 1 in 5 among Latino households (FDIC, 2014). Indeed, the unbanked are more likely to be

Hispanic, immigrant, low-income, and young (FDIC, 2014). To understand the context within which low-income, Latino, and immigrant families make financial choices about banking, we asked professionals working with the East Los Angeles Latino community to describe how community members save money and acquire assets. This article focuses on the community's relationship with banking institutions.

Literature review

Banking behavior results from a complex interplay of individual and contextual factors, as M. S. Sherraden's (2013) financial capability theory illustrates. Financial socialization, education, and guidance combine to give individuals the *knowledge* that guides their financial behavior. Yet knowledge by itself is insufficient to bring about financial stability and well-being. Individuals need financial inclusion, or access to financial *products* that are accessible, appropriate, affordable, financially attractive, and easy to use. Financial capability is achieved when the knowledge to act (financial literacy) combines with the opportunity to act (financial inclusion). This theory matches the reasons reported by unbanked individuals for not having a bank account, which include a blend of personal factors, such as not seeing the value of an account and disliking or distrusting banks, and structural factors, such as high minimum balances, insufficient money to open an account, high service fees, and lack of proper identification (Barr, 2008; FDIC, 2014; Bucks, Kennickell, & Moore, 2006; Seidman, Hababou, & Kramer, 2005).

Banks are taking some steps toward making their products more available to these potential consumers. FDIC's (2012) survey of banking practices reports that some banks are already lowering barriers to banking by accepting nontraditional forms of identification to open bank accounts, such as non-US passports, foreign consulate ID, and Individual Tax payer ID Number (ITIN). Many (37%) of the banks reported directly marketing to the unbanked and underbanked, and some (21%) reported making *second-chance* accounts available to consumers. This financial product enables clients to reenter the banking system after making financial mistakes. Many (43%) provided multilingual staff. Can banks do more to serve this population? Certainly, increasing the frequency of these accommodations would be a start (FDIC, 2012). Yet as Birkenmaier (2012) pointed out, banks are not designed to provide such services. Commercial banks are driven by profit considerations. They target higher-income clients and earn money from loans, fees, and trading activity. Because commercial banks do not profit from serving low-income consumers and business owners, such relationships are challenging for both parties.

Alternative Financial Services (AFS), in contrast, do much more to provide financial products to low-income and minority community members. AFS are offered by providers operating outside of federally insured depository institutions and services include short-term loans (payday loans, title loans, and pawning), check-cashing, and rent-to-own services (Bradley, Burnhouse, Gratton, & Miller, 2009). They cluster in low-income Hispanic and immigrant communities, as demonstrated by zip-code tabulation-area analysis across the United States (Burkey & Simkins, 2004; Fellowes & Mabanta, 2008; Gallmeyer & Roberts, 2009; Oron, 2006; Smith, Mosher, & Akins, 2006). AFS providers ease the use of credit products in these communities by providing households with poor or no credit, and those who face financial insecurity, with immediate access to funds, without facing the credit and background checks of traditional banking services (Barr, 2008; Fellowes & Mabanta, 2008). Yet these services come at a price: The average fee for payday loans is $15–20 per $100 borrowed, and fees amount to an annual percentage rate ranging from 391% to 521% (Center for Responsible Lending, 2009). Targeting the financially insecure in low-income communities is an essential part of the AFS business model. The majority (76%) of AFS loans are *churned*, which means that the client needed to take out another loan within a 2-week period to cover the shortfall in funds from repaying the previous loan; for many, the cost of the loans exceeds the original amount borrowed (Center for Responsible Lending, 2009).

If AFS products are so expensive and the AFS business model is fundamentally exploitative, what explains the community's claims that mistrust and the high cost of services keep them from utilizing traditional banking services (Barr, 2008; Bucks, Kennickell, & Moore, 2006; FDIC, 2014; Seidman et al., 2005)? Two explanations seem logical. One is that limited knowledge of formal financial practices among immigrant, low-income, and minority communities (Zhan, Anderson, & Scott, 2013) leaves them unaware of the benefits of banking. Another is that commercial banks' focus on higher-income households (Birkenmaier, 2012) may leave low-income households with few options that are suitable to their banking needs outside of AFS products.

The dichotomy turns out to be false. An individual from a low-income community of color has choices beyond the easily accessible but financially risky AFS products and the relatively inaccessible but potentially beneficial formal banking products (Birkenmaier, 2012). For-profit community banks and nonprofit credit unions are mission-driven to be of service to the community. This orientation often translates into lower-cost financial products and more flexibility in lending decisions. Unlike over half of the banks in the FDIC (2012) survey, community banks and credit unions tend to collaborate with nonprofits and community advocates, which have direct relationships with the community (Birkenmaier, 2012), suggesting that community members should have better access to the financial products of these organizations than to those of commercial banks.

The presence of agents who appear to be both accessible and financially salutary makes the persistence of low rates of banking in these communities that much more puzzling. This study seeks to find answers to this puzzle. Current research is unable to detect the interplay of institutional and individual factors within specific low-income, immigrant, Latino communities. The main body of research on the financial behavior of low-income individuals examines their use of asset-building products by evaluating associations between variables; this methodological approach cannot capture the interplay of these factors and connection to banking (Lincoln & Guba, 1985; Richards & Thyer, 2011). Qualitative studies exist (Hannagan & Morduch, 2015; Sherraden, McBride, & Beverly, 2010), but these still focus on the individual as the unit of analysis. To address this gap in the literature, our study uses qualitative methods to focus on a single community as the unit of analysis.

Methods

Research site and object of analysis

The object of inquiry is the East Los Angeles (ELA) community, as described by community experts (CEs). ELA is a continuous immigrant gateway (Singer, Hardwick, & Brettell, 2008). Although in the decades before WWII, Japanese and Jewish populations had also settled in this area (Benitez, 2004), it is currently overwhelmingly Latino (97.6%) and Mexican (89.2%) (U.S. Census Bureau, 2013). At the time of the study (2013–2014), demographically ELA was largely low-income, with many immigrants, low educational attainment, and low home ownership relative to Los Angeles, California, and the United States (see Table 1). The proportion of undocumented ELA immigrants is estimated to be high (Passel & Cohn, 2011).

Table 1. East Los Angeles community demographics in comparative perspective.

Demographics	East Los Angeles	California	United States
Population	127,897	37,253,956	308,745,538
Hispanic or Latino	124,855 (97.6%)	14,270,345 (38.3%)	51,786,591 (16.7%)
Foreign-born	54,851 (43.9%)	10,175,839 (27.3%)	40,341,898 (13.0%)
Median Household Income	$37,982	$61,094	$53,046
Persons Below Poverty Level	26.9%	15.9%	15.4%
Homeownership Rate	35.7%	55.9%	65.1%
Median Age	29.7	35.4	37.3
High School Graduate or Higher	45.6%	81.2%	86.0%

Participants

We collected information about ELA residents from 34 key informants from the community, called CEs (Fetterman, 2008). We defined CEs as individuals whose professional responsibilities brought them in direct contact with ELA residents (e.g., social workers), or who were responsible for making decisions about community programs based on their understanding of the community (e.g., a manager in a local credit union; see Table 2). We used purposive sampling to recruit CEs with expertise on ELA community members' financial transactions (i.e., management and front line staff in local banking and asset-building organizations). We then used convenience sampling to recruit CEs with minimal involvement in finances or asset-building, to ensure diversity of perspectives on the ELA community. Identities of individuals and organizations were kept confidential.

Data collection, analysis, and verification

Data collection

Using a team of graduate research assistants (RAs) trained in interview methods (Weiss, 1995), we conducted 36 in-depth (about one hour), semi-structured interviews, typically in CEs' place of work. No financial compensation was offered. RAs transcribed audio recordings and uploaded them to Dedoose, an online qualitative analysis program.

Data analysis

Throughout the implementation of the study, members of our research team created analytical memos to capture reflections both as they

Table 2. Participant characteristics (N = 34).

Characteristics	N	%
Inside asset-related field	24	70.5
from banking (commercial bank, credit union, community bank)	5	14.3
from asset-building programs targeting ELA low income (e.g., credit counselors)	10	29.4
from real estate firm targeting ELA vicinity	5	14.3
from financial assistance programs for ELA university students	4	11.4
Outside asset-related field (e.g., social worker, police officer, self-employed)	10	28.5
Origin		
Identify personal origin as from the community	11	32.3
Identify personal origin as from outside the community	11	32.3
Did not identify himself/herself	12	35.2
Hierarchy		
Directors	16	45.7
Front-line staff	19	54.3
Sectors		
Public	9	26.4
Non-profit	16	47
For profit (including self-employed)	9	26.5

occurred and in a structured fashion at key intervals (e.g., just after an interview or in preparation for a peer debriefing). After conducting sufficient interviews (about 10) to start noticing patterns in the data collected, we began to develop a codebook. Members of the research team independently developed codes for the same transcript, and the team subsequently worked together to synthesize the codes. We repeated this process until we reached consensus that the codebook captured important elements of the data. However, we assigned one code (*new code?*) to capture any new elements that appeared important. Once all interviews were conducted, the first and second authors used the same process (applying codes independently to the same transcript and then resolving inconsistencies together) to code the transcripts, until inconsistencies were negligible. At this point, the first author coded the remaining transcripts, with the second author reviewing the coding for all transcripts. We also used open-ended analytical notes during coding, to discern larger patterns in the data. The themes of mistrust and *word of mouth* began as analytical notes regarding potential themes, and repeated instances were added to the original analytical memo as they occurred. These two preliminary themes were selected because they were related to, by far, the greatest number of instances, relative to other open-ended analyses. The first author then recoded all the transcripts with the addition of these two codes, searching specifically for instances that would contradict the expected patterns and consulting with the second author frequently. All other themes reported here are drawn from the initial coding process (see Table 3). Information about community financial practice and knowledge was drawn from $ *strategies*, community outreach efforts were drawn from excerpts double-coded as $ *instruction* and *facilitation*, and evidence of strain was drawn from excerpts double-coded as $ *instruction* and *barriers*.

Table 3. Codebook excerpts.

Select codes related to this study				
Contextual Factors	Individual factors	Meta	Valance	Other
Asset-building field[1]	$ Instruction[3]	New code?	Facilitation	Mis/trust
General context[2]	$ Strategies[4]	Good quote	Barrier	"Word of mouth"
Banking		Unsure re coding	*Weight (1–3)* [5]	Undocumented
$ Exploitation				Towards policy[6]

Select definitions for less obvious codes
(1) How the field is structured. Who works with whom? Who funds whom?
(2) Other fields and regulations that indirectly impact asset acquisition
(3) Strategies individuals are *taught* regarding money management
(4) Strategies individuals actually *practice*
(5) Dedoose allows weighting. We used: (1) perfect exemplar, (2) appropriate, (3) a stretch
(6) Suggestions CEs would make for policy makers

Data verification

We used established, well-regarded techniques (Lincoln & Guba, 1985) to strengthen the credibility of the findings. *Prolonged engagement* refers to extensive time spent in the field. The majority of RAs entered the project with insider knowledge of ELA, having grown up in the community. Although an outsider to the community studied, the second author's residence to ELA since 2013, and collaboration with some CEs on financial empowerment projects following data collection for this study (e.g., developing new programs), grants her some access to their less formal observations about the ELA community. *Triangulation of sources* is evident in the diverse professional backgrounds of CEs interviewed; *triangulation of investigators* was achieved during the collection and preliminary analysis of the data. Specifically, *peer debriefing* was used to engage in rigorous questioning of preliminary findings. As the principal investigator, the second author peer debriefed with a faculty colleague from a related social work field over the course of the study, and presented preliminary findings to scholars in the asset-building field. *Negative case analysis*, the process of checking proposed themes against data collected, was also employed when recoding the data for the two new codes. Finally, we conducted a *member check*, presenting our findings to CEs from the study. The member check allowed participants to react to and adjust researchers' characterization of their reality, and produced one correction of emphasis: It appeared that we had underestimated the wariness with which CEs themselves regarded commercial banking establishments.

Findings

CEs reported that mistrust and misinformation about the financial system keeps ELA residents from accessing the banking system. CEs shared the strategies they have used to financially empower the community and noted that low levels of financial education can lead ELA residents to becoming unbankable. Systemic issues became evident.

(Mis)trust and (mis)information, amplified through social networks

It quickly became obvious, through repeated mention across the majority of the interviews, that ELA residents generally mistrust institutions. Frank, a Los Angeles police officer, suggested that experience and undocumented status fuel this fear and mistrust:

> A lot of them just have that common fear and mistrust of government or police agencies, based on their own personal experiences, and fear ... of maybe some sort of deportation, you know, if they were to disclose that they are here illegally.

A worker at a local community organization and resident of ELA, Jen, confirms the role of documentation in Frank's claim: "I think a lot of people are scared because they do not have documents, they are scared that they might get caught, taken back, and deported."

CEs described a similar fear and mistrust of banking institutions specifically, again linked to personal history and undocumented status. Peter, director of an asset-building organization, heard from an ELA client: "I have absolutely no trust in the financial system." Joseph, a community bank manager, reasoned that "many believe that if they open an account, their information will be reported to the government if they are undocumented." CEs also explained that many ELA residents had had negative experiences with financial institutions in their country of origin. Liana, an outreach coordinator of a commercial bank and resident of ELA, described her father's experience: "He went to a bank in Mexico to open an account and he put all his savings in there; when he came back ... to make a withdrawal, the bank said, 'What money? You don't have any money.'"

A minority of participants blamed practices of the financial sector, with the clearest example coming from Liana's explanation of the now-illegal practice of cashing incoming checks from largest to smallest, which depletes consumer accounts and provides banks with the opportunity to charge separate overdraft fees for any small transactions that follow. During the member check, CEs placed more emphasis on questionable motives of the financial sector. One example provided is that banks advertise in Spanish but provide related legal documents only in English. The California Reinvestment Coalition has long been waging a campaign against this practice, and CEs suggested that banks have few incentives to fund such translations. The final example comes from June, a research assistant and social worker from the ELA community who was interviewed after leaving the project. She described her experience with a credit card company: "[The phone operator] told me it was going to be interest free and I found out that it was not. I was very stressed ... crying, because I found out they were charging me really, really high interest." Although it is true that June may have been mistaken in the original call, one of the Consumer Financial Protection Bureau's red flags for unscrupulous lending is a salesperson who gives rates not supported in the documentation (Consumer Financial Protection Bureau, 2015).

The more typical examples of mistrust related to banking practices were rooted in misinformation about how the financial system actually functions. Liana shared that some clients do not understand the concept of overdraft: "[I] have some customers that say 'I got a fee, I don't know why I got a fee, you told me I wasn't going to.' I do explain to them ... but they have no idea what that [overdraft] is." She added that some clients do not understand why check deposit funds are not immediately available, despite explaining that banks holds funds from checks until they clear: "They don't understand it: 'This is my check, my work check, why can't you give me the money right now?'" As another example, Joseph explained that since the 2008 economic crash, ELA residents have watched banks foreclose on low-income families in the community who were not paying their mortgages, and it was not just the homeowners who were affected. Renting families were forced to move when property owners lost their mortgage. Joseph pointed out that banks had the right to foreclose; however, these actions still reinforced the opinion that banks were untrustworthy: "That process and the way it affected them further soured their relationship with the formal banking system, and it was, in their minds, just more evidence that banks are not good, and you have to look out for yourself."

CEs noted that experiences with the banking system occur on a personal level with ELA residents, but these experiences affect the larger community. They argued that communication, good or bad, is amplified through social networks and transmitted intergenerationally. Peter summarized that "the way many of our community members get the information to utilize [services] and make financial decisions … is through the trust of social networks." June provided her personal experience as an example: "I was working under the table … and a customer told me, 'Come to my bank … and bring your ID and you're fine' and I trusted him because I knew this guy; he was a client." Intergenerational transmission was even more frequently noted. As Joseph observed, "[Immigrants] come here and there is a general distrust of banks. So their kids grow up distrusting banks, and their kids' kids grow up distrusting banks." Liana also noted that knowledge of the financial system, or its lack, is passed to the next generation: "Sometimes their parents don't have the tools or the knowledge to teach them and when they become adults they kind of follow the same footsteps as their parents financially." June's background provides a specific example of Liana's point. June was born in the United States to an immigrant father who taught her to distrust banks and to use rent-to-own stores as a good way to build credit. Finally, on a more positive note, Irene, a supervisor at a local credit union, shared that personal communication has brought new clients to her credit union: "We get more new members just from word of mouth than anything else."

Many ELA residents make use of alternative methods to manage their money. It was very common for CEs to report that ELA residents keep their money at home, under the mattress or in a coffee pot. Some residents use *Tandas*, also known as lending circles, to borrow money, even though, as two CEs pointed out, these don't contribute to credit worthiness and are not considered safe. Some ELA residents also use AFS, and their use was a common concern among CEs from the banking and asset-building fields. Irene disclosed: "We saw so many of our members getting in trouble with these predatory payday lenders." Joy, a financial counsellor at a local asset-building organization, confirmed that some of her clients make use of AFS: "I do have a few, [a] handful of clients that have used, for example payday loans, those are just … just very expensive. They are very hard to get out of." Jen observed the convenience associated with the use of AFS products:

> People go there to buy tokens, to buy their bus passes, I mean it is a convenience store, but if you want to cash your check, that's when they charge you money and that is a bummer. $7 or $10 is money from your pocket. When you have a bank account you can get it for free.

Community-based organizations' efforts to help the unbanked become financially empowered

Given CEs' observations about the importance of trust in the ELA community and the potential amplification of messages through social relationships, CEs devote a lot of attention to establishing trust with the community as they deliver information. They consider developing trust with ELA residents to be essential for educating and guiding them into the formal financial system. Joy noted that one way of developing trust with community residents is to partner with stakeholders in the community: "We go out to different non-profits, different schools, and we start developing relationships with those entities." Joseph confirmed that he uses this same strategy:

> [We] work with those influences in the community, to get their trust, so they can work with their particular groups to encourage them to work with us. And even then, I mean, they do that but even then is still a struggle, but it is a little easier because they can reach out to 25, 50, 100, [a] thousand people at once, versus us having to deal with one, two, or three at a time.

CEs reported that part of building trust and empowering community residents involves deconstructing the fear of the banking system, explaining the importance of being banked, and explaining financial products and services so residents can understand how the financial system works. CEs use examples and concepts that relate to ELA residents' immediate experiences and connect opportunities to future goals. They discuss, for instance, that it is possible for undocumented individuals to open a bank account using ITIN numbers, passports from their country of origin, and the *matricula consular*. Joseph clarifies to residents that "[the law] requires that an individual who opens a bank account … provide a current government issue[d] form of identification with a photo, date of birth, and that has an expiration date on it." Liana added that one may need "a secondary ID, like a card with your name on it, [and] that's enough for you to open an account."

Because Joseph is aware that undocumented residents are afraid of being reported to the government by financial institutions, he explains to them why it is so unlikely for such a report to happen. According to him, the Financial

Privacy Act outlaws the sharing of individuals' financial information unless there is suspicion of criminal activity in an account, in which case government agencies must provide a subpoena that allows a *targeted* search. Joseph then uses the fear of deportation as an argument *for* becoming banked:

> When you keep your assets in the form of cash, in a mattress or in a cookie jar … it is very susceptible to theft, very susceptible to damage. … We do have a large population that is undocumented, to the extent that [if] they become deported … it [cash] can be lost. … Versus, if it is at a bank, it really doesn't matter what your documentation status is; that money is insured and protected for you. … Now if the worst happens and you are deported in the middle of the night, that money remains secure, safe, and insured here. You can ask us to send it to you abroad, or wherever you might be across the border.

Because CEs recognize the important connection between banking and asset acquisition, they are concerned, as Peter reflects, that "[they] don't understand that if they don't document that income … in the long term [they] are building barriers … to access finances to build a business or a home … your kid's education or something else." Thus, Liana, for instance, explains to her customers that making one's income and payments visible via a checking account is important because "later on when they come to ask for a loan, especially a home loan, if you can't track your payments and you can't prove that you have been making your payments, you didn't make them."

CEs also recognize that empowering ELA residents involves teaching them how the financial system works at the quotidian level. Liana reported, for instance, that she clarifies the difference between checking and savings accounts, debit and credit cards, and that she also translates the concept of overdraft fee: "Let's say you have $10 in your account and you go and … spend $20, the bank may say, 'Ok [we] will give you the small loan of $10 … but as an interest we are going to charge you $35.'" She also explains to clients the importance of building credit: "[I] tell my customers, 'This country runs on credit. … You have to have credit to have … an apartment, for everything, because that is who you are on paper when you apply for any loan, or anything." But she also warns clients that if they obtain a credit card, they should choose one with no annual fee, and should only pay ongoing expenses with it and limit their use to 30%–50% of their credit line, to show restraint with their finances: "[I] tell customers … 'You have a cell phone right?' 'Yes, I do.' 'And you pay it every month?' 'Yes, I do.' 'Ok, so get a credit card, pay your cell phone [with it] and the next day pay your credit card.'"

Joy reported that she sits with her clients and explains the different checking account options offered by financial institutions in the community, so that clients can make an educated decision when looking to open a banking account:

We are trying to help them understand "these are your options. ... We want to make sure you open the right bank account, not a bank account that is going to charge you because that defeats the whole purpose." So it's offering them options, "Ok, so bank A, they accept ITIN but they are going to charge you if you do not maintain [a certain amount]."

Diego, another supervisor at a local credit union, reported that he instructs residents about budgeting and saving during his workshops: "I want to help them see ... how they can go ahead and save money." CEs often offer workshops in the community, and they noted that offering a series of workshops is more useful than offering a single one, giving them more time to cover all this information and to build rapport with ELA residents.

From unbanked to unbankable

CEs' attempts to financially empower ELA residents also suggest the process by which low levels of financial education can eventually bring individuals from being banked to becoming unbankable. Joseph pointed out that if ELA residents access the banking system but are not provided with adequate financial education, they may be at risk of misusing their accounts and being reported to the ChexSystems*, a consumer credit reporting agency, and consequently being locked out of the banking system. Liana described a client who was shut out from the financial system:

> I had a specific customer that would lay tile, that was his job, he had his own company; one of the people that he laid tile for gave him a $5,000 check. He deposited it and then it came back, but he had already used the money. He owed the bank that money and he didn't have that money to pay it back. He went back to the person who gave him the check, but he couldn't find him ... so his account was closed by the fraud department.

Joy also observed that "a lot of the clients coming in, they were in the ChexSystems*."

Joseph explained that once an individual is reported to ChexSystems*, "if these individuals try to open an account elsewhere, they are not going to be able to open the account. So ... [they] are forced into alternative financial services providers." Liana agreed with Joseph's view that being locked out of the banking system pushes individuals to utilize AFS to meet their financial needs.

It can be difficult to recover from becoming unbankable. Liana noted that in her bank "if you owe money to the bank at some point, you will not be able to qualify [for second-chance accounts]." Joy observed that this can even impede individuals from participating in asset-building programs that provide financial education. She shared that the organization she works for was partnering with a local financial institution to offer a matched savings program to ELA residents, to promote financial literacy and saving behavior. However, clients who had been previously reported to ChexSystems[*] were refused participation by the partnering financial institution: "There was no room for flexibility; no room for negotiating; no options for them."

The larger systemic issue of misinformation underlying the process of becoming unbankable is illuminated by Liana's observation that financial education is not included in California's school curriculum. She is often asked by high school teachers to provide financial workshops at the local high schools because "[students] are getting ready to go to college and they need an account and never had one. They have no idea what a debit card is." Such systemic issues appear connected to the sense of strain that seemed evident in CEs' descriptions of their attempts to empower the community. From his community banking perspective, Joseph shared that:

> It really requires a significant effort ... it's a very arduous process. These individuals are high-touch individuals, in other words, you need to really hold their hands a lot, you need to provide the financial literacy education, you need to monitor them to make sure they won't make the same mistakes over again. And so, when you do this at a scale of significant size, it becomes a pretty expensive proposition for a financial institution.

Diego similarly reflected that it is difficult to get community members to attend his educational seminars because many do not know what a credit union is. From the perspective of a CE at an asset-building organization, Joy explained that they do outreach and market their services in ELA, but because they are a nonprofit, they have time and funding constraints that limit their flexibility to perform these activities, and they have to rely heavily on word of mouth.

Discussion

Limitations

Before reflecting on this study's findings, its limitations should be noted. First, the sample size was small. In part, this is because the population of persons who are responsible for handling the needs of a specific community (e.g., the community outreach coordinator of a bank) is also small. Nevertheless, the results may have been broader or more robust if more agents and agencies had been included. In addition, the uniqueness of the study site should be kept in mind; it has an unusually high Latino population, a large and replenishing immigrant base, a considerable number of underdocumented individuals, and a low average income, all within a major urban center with a high cost of living. Replication of the study in ethnic enclaves of similar density and economic standing, or in communities with members whose everyday activities are constrained by legal status issues, would help to determine the theoretical generalizability of the findings to other low-income immigrant populations (Lincoln & Guba, 1985; Luker, 2008). Additionally, the diversity of practices and mind-sets among community members is not fully reflected in this study of general trends.

Discussion

The evidence suggests cooccurring trends in this community: the amplification of both mistrust and miseducation through social networks and down the generations. These stem from the undocumented and immigrant status of a sufficient number of community members, which give rise to fear and mistrust of institutions. Such is the dynamic that institutions of asset-building nonprofits and community banks face as they attempt to combat financial exploitation in their community. Given insufficient funding to advertise their calls for financial empowerment CEs seemed to take pride in their work while simultaneously acknowledging its Sisyphean nature. The results of this study dovetail with financial capability theory in suggesting that a comprehensive approach is needed to reverse apparent trends within typical ELA households, which either remain unbanked or, worse, move from unbanked to unbankable.

Conclusion

Considerable potential exists for intervening with ELA community at a scope commensurate to the problem. Although a systematic promotion of financial literacy through the school system in California, does not, at the time of this writing, exist, a law mandating financial curriculum in California was passed (Common Cents Curriculum Act of 2013), and school curricula are to be slowly changed as a result. Although social workers are not yet being trained in finances, there are some recent advances toward such training. The legislation provides the opportunity to weave financial products with promotion of literacy in schools and social services in the community. For example, ELA's strong program of college promotion through primary schools could embed seeded college savings accounts. Infusing seeded college saving accounts to such a program would amplify the expectation that children are meant to go to college (Beverly, Elliott, & Sherraden, 2013; Sherraden, 1991) while simultaneously providing families with an asset-building product within the formal banking sector (Sherraden, 2013). Social workers could be trained to ask about these accounts when working with families; such accounts provide them with natural entry point into larger conversation about financial products and services provided in the community (Consumer

Financial Protection Bureau, 2015). Immigration issues add an additional layer of complexity to the already difficult interplay between low-income consumers and financial services. Mandatory financial education for youth combined with asset-building financial products is an example of an approach with sufficient scope to draw the community to potentially safer banking services.

Acknowledgments

This research was supported in part by The John Randolph Haynes and Dora Haynes Foundation. We also thank Dr. M. Elana Delavega for coining unbankable, our reviewers for thoughtful feedback, and most of all our participants and their institutions for their valuable time

References

Barr, M. S. (2008). *Financial services, savings and borrowing among low- and moderate-income households: Evidence from the Detroit Area Household Financial Services Survey* (SSRN Scholarly Paper No. ID 1121195). Rochester, NY: Social Science Research Network.

Benitez, T. (2004). *East L.A.: Past and present.* Retrieved from http://www.pbs.org/american family/eastla.html

Beverly, S., Elliott, W., & Sherraden, M. W. (2013). *Child Development Accounts and college success: Accounts, assets, expectations, and achievements.* Retrieved from https://csd.wustl. edu/Publications/Documents/P13-27.pdf

Birkenmaier, J. M. (2012). Promoting bank accounts to low-income households: Implications for social work practice. *Journal of Community Practice, 20,* 414–431. doi:10.1080/ 10705422.2012.732004

Bradley, C., Burnhouse, S., Gratton, H., & Miller, R. (2009). Alternative financial services: A primer. *FDIC Quarterly, 1*(3), 39–47.

Brooks, J., Wiedrich, K., Sims, L.Jr.,, & Rice, S. (2015). *Excluded from the financial main-stream: How the economic recovery is bypassing millions of Americans.* Washington, DC: CFED. Retrieved from cfed.gov

Bucks, B. K., Kennickell, A. B., & Moore, K. B. (2006). Recent changes in U.S. family finances: Evidence from the 2001 and 2004 Survey of Consumer Finances. *Federal Reserve Bulletin, 92,* A1–A38. Retrieved from http://www.federalreserve.gov/econresdata/scf/scf_2004.htm

Burkey, M. L., & Simkins, S. P. (2004). Factors affecting the location of payday lending and traditional banking services in North Carolina. *Review of Regional Studies, 34,* 191–205. Retrieved from https://mpra.ub.uni-muenchen.de/36043/1/MPRA_paper_36043.pdf

Center for Responsible Lending. (2009). *Phantom demand: Short term due date generates need for repeat payday loans, accounting for 76% of total volume.* Retrieved from http://www. responsiblelending.org/payday-lending/research-analysis/phantom-demand-final.pdf

Center for Responsible Lending. (2015). *Payday mayday: Visible and invisible payday lending defaults.* Retrieved from http://www.responsiblelending.org

Common Cents Curriculum Act, Cal. Assemb. A.B. 166 (2013), Chapter 135 (Cal. Stat. 2013).

Consumer Financial Protection Bureau. (2015). *Your money, your goals: A financial empow-erment toolkit for social services programs.* Retrieved from http://files.consumerfinance.gov/ f/201407_cfpb_your-money-your-goals_toolkit_english.pdf

Federal Deposit Insurance Corporation. (2012). *2011 FDIC survey of banks efforts' to serve the unbanked and underbanked.* Retrieved from https://www.fdic.gov/unbankedsurveys/

Federal Deposit Insurance Corporation. (2014). *2013 FDIC National survey of unbanked and underbanked households.* Retrieved from http://www.fdic.gov/householdsurvey/2013_unbankedreport.pdf

Fellowes, M., & Mabanta, M. (2008). *Banking on wealth: America's new retail banking infrastructure and its wealth-building potential.* Washington, DC: The Brookings Institution, Metropolitan Policy Program. Retrieved from https://www.brookings.edu/wp-content/uploads/2016/06/01_banking_fellowes.pdf

Fetterman, D. M. (2008) Key informants. In L. M. Given (Ed.), *The SAGE encyclopedia of qualitative research methods* (pp. 477–478). Thousand Oaks, CA: Sage Publications. Retrieved from http://knowledge.sagepub.com/view/research/SAGE.xml

Gallmeyer, A., & Roberts, W. T. (2009). Payday lenders and economically distressed communities: A spatial analysis of financial predation. *The Social Science Journal, 46*, 521–538. doi:10.1016/j.soscij.2009.02.008

Hannagan, A., & Morduch, J. (2015). *Income gains and month-to-month income volatility: Household evidence from the US Financial Diaries.* Retrieved from http://www.usfinancialdiaries.org/paper-1

Lincoln, Y. S., & Guba, E. G. (1985). *Naturalistic inquiry.* Newbury Park, CA: Sage.

Luker, K. (2008). *Salsa dancing into the social sciences: Research in an age of info-glut.* Cambridge, MA: Harvard University Press.

Oron, A. (2006). *Easy prey: Evidence for race and military related targeting in the distribution of pay-day loan branches in Washington state.* Seattle, WA: Department of Statistics, University of Washington. Retrieved from http://www.docstoc.com/docs/164745589/Easy-Prey

Passel, J., & Cohn, D. (2011). *Unauthorized immigrant population: National and state trends, 2010.* Pew Research Center. Retrieved from http://www.pewhispanic.org/2011/02/01/unauthorized-immigrant-population-brnational-and-state-trends-2010/

Pew Research Center. (2011). *Wealth gaps rise to record highs between Whites, Blacks and Hispanics.* Retrieved from http://www.pcwsocialtrends.org/2011/07/26/wealth-gaps-rise-to-record-highs-between-whites-blacks-hispanics/

Richards, K. V., & Thyer, B. A. (2011). Does Individual Development Account participation help the poor? A review. *Research on Social Work Practice, 21*, 348–362. doi:10.1177/1049731510395609

Seidman, E., Hababou, M., & Kramer, J. (2005). *A financial services survey of low- and moderate-income households.* Chicago, IL: Center for Financial Services Innovation. Retrieved from http://www.cfsinnovation.com/sites/default/files/imported/managed_documents/threecitysurvey.pdf

Sherraden, M. (1991). *Assets and the poor: A new American welfare policy.* Armonk, NY: M.E. Sharpe.

Sherraden, M. S. (2013). Building blocks of financial capability. In J. Birkenmaier, J. Curley, & M. Sherraden (Eds.), *Financial capability and asset development* (pp. 3–43). New York, NY: Oxford University Press.

Sherraden, M. S., McBride, A. M., & Beverly, S. G. (2010). *Striving to save: Creating policies for financial security of low-income families.* Ann Arbor, MI: University of Michigan Press.

Singer, A., Hardwick, S. W., & Brettell, C. (2008). *Twenty-first-century gateways: Immigrant incorporation in suburban America.* Washington, DC: Brookings Institution Press.

Smith, C. L., Mosher, C., & Akins, S. (2006). *Outsourcing the company store: Predatory lending in Washington State.* Paper presented at the Annual Meeting of the American

Sociological Association, Montreal, Canada. Retrieved from http://citation.allacademic. com/meta/p104576_index.html

U.S. Census Bureau. (2013). *2009–2013 American community survey 5-year estimates.* Retrieved from http://factfinder.census.gov/faces/tableservices/jsf/pages/productview. xhtml?src=CF

Weiss, R. S. (1995). *Learning from strangers: The art and method of qualitative interview studies* (1st ed.). New York, NY: Free Press.

Zhan, M., Anderson, S. G., & Scott, J. (2013). Improving financial capacity among low-income immigrants: Effects of a financial education program. In J. Birkenmaier, J. Curley, & M. Sherraden (Eds.), *Financial capability and asset development* (pp. 3–43). New York, NY: Oxford University Press.

Ethnic Differences in Financial Outcomes Among Low-Income Older Asian Immigrants: A Financial Capability Perspective

Yunju Nam, Jin Huang, and Eun Jeong Lee

ABSTRACT

This exploratory study examined ethnic differences in financial outcomes among low-income older Asian immigrants from a financial capability perspective. We used survey data collected from a convenience sample of Chinese, Korean, and "Other Asian" ethnic participants in a subsidized employment program ($n = 159$). We ran logit regressions of dichotomous financial outcomes. Regression analysis showed significant ethnic differences in some financial outcomes after controlling for financial capability and other factors. Findings did not support our hypothesis that financial capability explains ethnic differences in financial outcomes. Findings suggest the need to develop culturally suitable financial capability measures for future research.

Asian Americans have been the fastest-growing racial group in the United States for more than a decade, with a population growth rate of 46% between 2000 and 2010, higher than that of Hispanics (Asian Americans Advancing Justice, 2011). The population growth rate of Asian Americans is even higher among those 55 years old or older, at a rate of 85% between 2000 and 2010 (National Asian Pacific Center on Aging, 2013). Consequently, Asian Americans comprise an increasing proportion of the older adult population in the United States. The percentage of Asian Americans among older adults was 4.1% in 2014 (authors' calculation based on a table created by the US Census Bureau, 2015) and is projected to grow to 8.5% in 2050 (Federal Interagency Forum on Aging-Related Statistics, 2012; He, Sengupta, Velkoff, & DeBarros, 2005).

Despite the increasing size of this population, there has been relatively little research about their financial conditions and long-term economic security to date. This lack of inquiry may be a result of the so-called *model minority* myth, which encourages the public to view Asian Americans as an economically successful and socially problem-free population who do not need government assistance (Bascara, 2008). Empirical evidence, however, shows that Asian Americans face various challenges, including discriminatory treatment in the labor market and financial sectors (Hurh & Kim, 1989; Sakamoto, Goyette, & Kim, 2009). Another problem with the model minority stereotype is that it treats Asian Americans as a homogeneous group, when Asian Americans are composed of diverse subgroups with unique cultural values, historical experiences, and socioeconomic positions (Hurh & Kim, 1989).

This exploratory study investigates ethnic differences in financial capabilities and financial outcomes among low-income older Asian immigrants. A new theoretical framework of financial capability suggests that one's financial capability affects one's financial outcomes (Huang, Nam, & Sherraden, 2013; Sherraden, 2013). Based on this framework, the concept of financial capability in this study has two essential components: financial literacy (individual ability to act, which results in optimal financial outcomes) and financial access (institutional arrangements that provide financial services essential for long-term financial security; Sherraden, 2013). In measuring financial literacy, this study includes knowledge of two social programs (Social Security and Medicare) in addition to financial knowledge and financial management. Social Security and Medicare are "the bedrock of financial security" (Gould & Cooper, 2013, p. 3) for older Americans and, therefore, knowledge of these programs is critical for long-term financial planning among older adults (Nam, Lee, Huang, & Kim, 2015). This study defines financial outcomes as economic well-being indicators related to long-term economic security, such as asset accumulation, asset ownership, and retirement confidence. This study defines immigrants as foreign-born individuals who were permitted to live in the country permanently, following the Office of Immigration Statistics (Congressional Budget Office, 2004).

Background

According to the theoretical framework of financial capability, financial literacy and financial access are two essential components of long-term financial success. *Financial literacy* refers to an individual's ability to make decisions and act to improve long-term financial prospects. Financial literacy is composed of financial knowledge and financial management. Another component of financial capability, *financial access* is the access to financial products and services essential for long-term financial security. In summary, financial literacy is the individual's capability to act, and financial access is the institutional arrangement that provides the opportunity to act (Huang et al., 2013; Sherraden, 2013).

A small but increasing number of empirical studies support the financial capability framework. Financial literacy is associated positively with retirement planning (Lusardi & Mitchell, 2007) and wealth accumulation (Behrman, Mitchell, Soo, & Bravo, 2010), although it has a negative association with the use of high-cost loans and excessive indebtedness (Lusardi & Tufano, 2009). As a relatively new concept, financial access has little empirical evidence. In one of the few studies on the topic, Huang and colleagues (2013) demonstrated that both individual financial knowledge and access to Child Development Accounts had a positive impact on mothers' participation in a college savings program.

The theoretical framework of financial capability has the potential to explain group disparities in financial outcomes. Existing empirical studies have demonstrated substantial wealth disparities by race (Shanks & Leigh, 2015; Taylor, Kochhar, Fry, Velasco, & Motel, 2011), ethnicity (Hao, 2007), immigration status (Cobb-Clark & Hildebrand, 2006; Nam, 2014, 2015; Sevak & Schmidt, 2007), and gender (Chang, 2012; Denton & Boos, 2007). Differences in socioeconomic characteristics (e.g., education and family structure), however, do not fully explain wealth gaps (Borjas, 2002; Cobb-Clark & Hildebrand, 2006). As shown in Figure 1, it may be that different levels of financial literacy and access contribute to disparities in wealth and other financial outcomes. For example, ethnic wealth disparities among Asian immigrants (Hao, 2007) may be attributed to the different financial infrastructures in their countries of origin: Immigrants from countries with strong financial infrastructure are more likely to trust financial institutions and tend to participate in the US financial market more extensively than those from countries with weak infrastructure (Osili & Paulson, 2008). Financial knowledge may differ by ethnicity because of different financial experience at countries of origin, ethnic mass media, and ethnic communities. Approaches to financial management are likely influenced by ethnic values and culture and experience in the countries of origin. Ethnic wealth gaps may also be explained by expanded financial access provided by ethnic banks and informal financial institutions (e.g.,

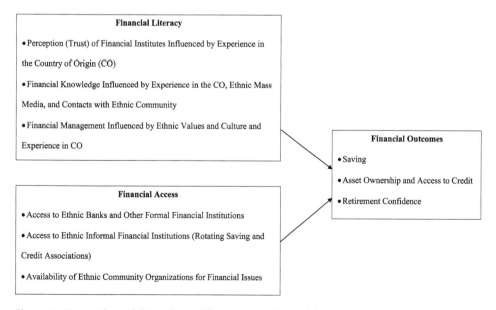

Figure 1. Financial capability, ethnic differences, and financial outcomes.

rotating saving and credit associations) that are only available to certain ethnic groups (Li, 2014; Moya, 2005).

Building on the financial capability framework and existing empirical studies (Hao, 2007; Huang et al., 2013; Nam et al., 2015), this study investigates ethnic differences in financial capability and financial outcomes among low-income older Asian immigrants. This study asks the following questions: (a) Are there differences in financial outcomes among Chinese, Koreans, and "Other Asian" ethnic groups? (b) Does financial capability have significant associations with financial outcomes? And (c) Does financial capability explain ethnic differences in financial outcomes?

Methods

Data and sample

This study used survey data collected from low-income older Asian immigrants in the National Asian Pacific Center on Aging's (NAPCA's) Senior Community Service Employment Program (SCSEP). NAPCA is a nonprofit organization that serves and advocates for older Asian Americans and Pacific Islanders. NAPCA runs a subsidized employment program (SCSEP) funded by the Department of Labor. SCSEP offers subsidized community service experiences and job training for low-income older adults (55 years old or older with a family income lower than 125% of the federal poverty guideline). SCSEP's eligibility rules allow only US citizens and permanent residents in the program. The majority of NAPCA's SCSEP participants are Asian immigrants although the program is open to non-Asians and native citizens.

We conducted the survey in March 2012, using a self-administered group survey method. We developed the survey questionnaire first in English, translated it into Chinese and Korean, and then back-translated the questionnaires into English to check the accuracy of the translated versions. We chose three survey locations out of NAPCA's nine SCSEP sites: Los Angeles (LA) and Orange County (OC) in California and New York City (NYC) in New York. We chose the LA and NYC sites because they have larger numbers of participants than other sites and selected the OC site because of its geographic proximity to LA to reduce survey cost. At the three sites, bilingual survey administrators conducted the survey with those who attended SCSEP's quarterly mandatory meetings. After explaining the study and informing them of their right to not participate, survey administrators asked study participants to fill out the survey and collected completed questionnaires. The Social and Behavioral Science Institutional Review Board at the University at Buffalo approved the design of the survey (Study # 4759).

At the time of the survey, a total of 220 SCSEP participants attended the meetings and 183 filled out the questionnaire (83% response rate). Among these

183 cases, we included Asian immigrants who filled out the survey questionnaire in English, Chinese, or Korean. We excluded 23 cases because they did not meet qualifications of survey participants (e.g., non-immigrants or non-Asians). Because of SCSEP eligibility rules, the sample included only US citizens and permanent residents. We also dropped one case that did not report his/her ethnicity from the analysis sample. The analysis sample contained 159 cases.

Measures

Dependent variables: financial outcomes

We used various dichotomous measures of financial outcomes: financial confidence, asset accumulation, asset ownership, access to credit, and retirement confidence. First, financial confidence was measured with respondents' comfort level in opening a bank account (1 for those who answered *very comfortable* or *somewhat comfortable* in opening a bank account and 0 for those who answered *very uncomfortable* or *somewhat uncomfortable*; Nam et al., 2015). Second, asset accumulation was measured with an indicator of saving regularly (1 for those who reported that they saved a regular amount each month and 0 for the others; Nam et al., 2015). Third, we created two indicators of asset ownership: bank account (1 for those reported that they or anyone in their household had a checking or savings account and 0 for the others) and long-term savings (1 for respondents who answered that they owned one of the following types of assets: savings account; money market account or certificate of deposit; retirement account; stocks or stock mutual funds; and corporate, municipal, government, or foreign bonds; and 0 for the others; Nam et al., 2015). Fourth, access to credit was measured as possession of a major credit card (1 for respondents who reported to have a credit card and 0 otherwise), because credit cards provide an easy and immediate access to credit by permitting individuals to carry a balance (Nam et al., 2015). Last, retirement confidence was measured with a question selected from the Employee Benefit Research Institute's (2003) Minority Retirement Confidence Survey. This variable assigned 1 to those who were *very confident* or *somewhat confident* that they had "enough money to take care of basic expenses throughout retirement years" and 0 for the others.

Main independent variable: ethnicity

The ethnicity variable was created based on respondents' own reports. This variable is composed of three categories: Chinese or Taiwanese, Korean, and "Other Asian" (e.g., Asian Indian, Filipino).

Demographic, human capital, and citizenship variables

This study included several demographic variables: the respondent's age (1 for *65 years old and older* and 0 for *younger than 65*); gender (1 for *female* and 0 for *male*); marital status (1 for *currently married* and 0 for *others*); and household size (only one person; two people; and three or more). Human capital variables included education attainment (less than a high school diploma; a high school diploma; and a bachelor's degree or higher); work experience in the United States (1 for those with *10 or more years of experience*; 0 for the *others*); English proficiency (1 for those who answered that they spoke English *somewhat* or *very well*; 0 for the others). The citizenship variable indicated whether a respondent was currently a US citizen or not.

Financial capability

We included three types of financial capability variables: knowledge, management, and access. We measured two types of knowledge: financial knowledge and social program knowledge. The first measure, the financial knowledge scale, summed the number of right answers to true-or-false questions on four basic financial issues: benefits of long-term savings, interest rates, credit ratings, and credit and debt management. Examples of these questions included: "All banks give you the same rate of interest on your savings accounts" and "Your credit rating is not affected by how much you charge on your credit cards." We selected these questions after reviewing multiple large-scale surveys (e.g., the Health and Retirement Study and the Survey of Consumers). In addition, financial issues included in these four questions are consistent with three of five financial knowledge core competencies proposed by the US Financial Literacy and Education Commission (US Department of Treasury, 2010). Finally, this approach has been used by existing research to evaluate participants' financial knowledge (e.g., Huang et al., 2013; Lusardi & Mitchell, 2007). The financial knowledge scale ranged between 0 and 4 and its Cronbach's alpha was estimated to be 0.71 in the sample. The social program knowledge scale measured knowledge of Social Security and Medicare because these social programs play a crucial role in older adults' economic security. The scale counted the number of correct answers to five true-or-false questions about Social Security and Medicare, such as "Your Social Security benefit amount will be the same regardless of age of retirement." The potential range of this scale was between 0 and 5, and its Cronbach's alpha was 0.75 in the sample. The financial management variable asked respondents whether they regularly tracked their spending, with a choice of the following options: *often true* (2); *sometimes true* (1); and *rarely true* (0). This approach to measuring financial management was taken from the Saving for Education, Entrepreneurship and Downpayment Pre-School Demonstration and Impact Assessment (Beverly, 2006). Financial access was measured by respondents' own evaluation of their ease in speaking with bank staff members (1 for those who *strongly agree* or *agree* that "it is easy to speak with bank staff members" and 0 for the others).

Analytical approaches

We employed a multiple imputation method that is estimated to be one of the best approaches in dealing with missing cases (Schafer & Graham, 2002). The number of missing cases in the sample ranged from 1 (work experience) to 51 (keeping track of spending). Dropping these missing cases would have reduced the analysis sample size and would have brought estimation bias if these cases differed systematically from those with complete information. As a simulation-based approach in dealing with missing data issues, multiple imputation consists of three steps: (a) imputation (creating multiple completed datasets by imputing missing values based on an imputation model), (b) estimation (data analysis using completed data generated at the imputation step), and (c) pooling (combining results from multiple estimation steps using multiple completed data sets into a single multiple-imputation result; Little & Rubin, 2002; Schafer & Graham, 2002; STATACorp, 2009). The goal of multiple imputation is not to impute individual missing values close to their true values, but to generate valid statistical inference for the analysis of interest (Little & Rubin, 2002; Schafer & Graham, 2002). Although multiple imputation is based on the assumption of missing at random, the impacts of the violation of this assumption on estimates and standard errors are rarely substantial in many realistic cases of multiple imputation analyses (Schafer & Graham, 2002). For each analysis, we used 30 imputations, as Schafer and Graham (2002) recommend using 20 or more imputations to eliminate noise from the estimate.

Because the dependent variables were dichotomous, we used logit regressions at the estimation step. We employed three models for each dependent variable. The first model included the ethnicity dummy variables and assessed an overall difference among the three groups. The second model added demographic, human capital, and citizenship variables to the first model. The comparisons of ethnicity variables between the two models enabled us to see whether observed ethnic differences in model 1 were explained with these variables. The third model was comprehensive, with financial capability variables added to those in the second model. This model showed the roles of financial capability variables in explaining ethnic differences in financial outcomes.

We did not include earnings, family income, or survey locations in our analyses. There was little variation in earnings among respondents: SCSEP pays local minimum wage to all participants, and all respondents reported that they worked 20 hours a week. Because of SCSEP income eligibility rules, variations in family income were small. We excluded the survey location variable because the number of respondents at the OC site was small ($n = 26$), and the results from a model with the location variable were not substantially different from those reported in this article. (The full results of the supplemental analyses are available from the authors.)

Findings

Bivariate analyses: sample characteristics and financial outcomes by ethnicity

Table 1 compares demographics, human capital, citizenship, financial capability, and financial outcomes by ethnicity. The sample consisted of 51 Chinese (32%), 62 Koreans (39%), and 46 "Other Asian" ethnic group members (29%). Table 1 clearly shows ethnic differences in the sample. The Chinese respondents were significantly younger and more likely to be married than the other two groups. Korean respondents were significantly more likely to have 10 or more years of work experience in the United States than the other two groups. The "Other Asian"

Table 1. Sample characteristics and financial outcomes by ethnicity.

	Chinese	Korean	"Other Asian"
Sample composition	51 (32.08%)	62 (38.99%)	46 (28.93%)
Demographics			
Age, 65 or older[a,b]	39.22%	54.84%	69.57%
Female[a]	47.06%	62.90%	58.70%
Married[a,b]	72.55%	56.45%	54.35%
Household size: one person	17.65%	30.65%	17.39%
two people	54.90%	46.77%	30.43%
three or more	27.45%	22.58%	52.17%
Education: less than high school	17.65%	12.10%	19.93%
high school diploma	52.94%	41.02%	42.39%
BA or more	29.41%	46.88%	37.68%
10+ work experience[b,c]	47.06%	53.23%	26.45%
Good English[a,b,c]	23.53%	38.71%	69.57%
Citizen[c]	52.94%	60.00%	42.03%
Financial capability			
Financial knowledge (Mean)[a]	0.78	1.23	0.98
Social program knowledge (Mean)	2.29	2.24	1.89
Keeping track spending[b,c]: rarely	33.46%	36.24%	15.94%
sometimes	28.24%	37.31%	41.59%
often	38.30%	26.45%	42.46%
Ease w/bank staff	89.35%	93.98%	81.01%
Financial Outcomes			
Comfortable in opening a bank account[b]	86.67%	76.72%	62.17%
Regularly save	15.69%	11.29%	21.74%
Banked[a,b]	94.12%	72.58%	73.91%
Long-term savings[a,b]	54.90%	24.19%	30.43%
Credit card	45.10%	33.87%	39.13%
Retirement confident[b,c]	16.27%	21.88%	41.30%

[a] The difference between Chinese and Korean is significant at the 0.1 level.
[b] The difference between Chinese and "Other Asians" is significant at the 0.1 level.
[c] The difference between Korean and "Other Asian" is significant at the 0.1 level.

ethnic respondents' English proficiency was better than that of the other two groups, probably because many of them came from English-speaking countries, such as the Philippines and India. In terms of financial capability, Koreans had the best financial knowledge, but showed the worst financial management practices: Only a quarter reported that they often kept track of spending. Differences in financial management were significant between Koreans and the other two groups.

Table 1 also compares financial outcomes among the three ethnic groups. First, Chinese respondents showed a significantly higher rate of being comfortable in opening a bank account than "Other Asian" ethnic respondents (87% and 62%, respectively, $p < 0.05$). The percentages of respondents who reported regularly saving were very low among all three groups (22% "Other Asian" ethnic group, 16 % Chinese, and 11% Koreans). Differences between the three groups were not statistically significant. Chinese respondents were significantly more likely to have a bank account and long-term savings than the other two groups. Credit card ownership was highest among Chinese respondents (45%), followed by "Other Asian" (39%) and Koreans (34%). Retirement confidence was low for all three groups (16% among Chinese, 22% among Koreans, and 41% among "Other Asian").

In addition, we compared the rates of ownership for various types of assets between those who reported that they saved regularly and those who reported they did not because these variables may be highly correlated to each other. The former were not significantly more likely to have a bank account, home, or credit card than the latter. The two groups significantly differed at the 0.1 level only for long-term savings ownership (52% and 33%, respectively). Low levels of association between the asset accumulation and asset ownership variables justified separate analyses for financial outcome variables. (Full analysis results are available from the authors.)

Regression analysis results

Table 2 shows logit regression results for two financial outcome measures: being comfortable in opening a bank account and saving regularly. The first column (Model 1) in Table 2 reports that "Other Asian" respondents were significantly less likely to be comfortable with opening a bank account than Chinese respondents. In Model 2, the coefficient of "Other Asian" lost its statistical significance. This result suggests that the difference between Chinese and "Other Asian" ethnic groups may be explained by differences in demographic, human capital, and citizenship variables. Similarly, neither ethnic dummy variable was statistically significant in Model 3. Table 3 also shows a large and statistically significant coefficient of the measure of financial access, suggesting those who reported it was easy to speak with bank staff members were more likely to feel comfortable in opening a bank account.

Table 2. Logit regression on opening a bank account and regular saving.

	Comfortable with Bank			Regularly Save		
	Model 1	Model 2	Model 3	Model 1	Model 2	Model 3
Korean	−0.71	−0.71	−0.80	−0.38	−0.47	−0.37
Standard error	(0.64)	(0.68)	(0.75)	(0.56)	(0.62)	(0.66)
p-value	0.27	0.30	0.29	0.50	0.44	0.58
"Other Asian"	−1.41*	−1.12	−1.00	0.40	0.30	0.47
Standard error	(0.62)	(0.71)	(0.81)	(0.53)	(0.66)	(0.72)
p-value	0.02	0.12	0.22	0.45	0.65	0.51
65 or older		0.05	−0.10		−0.07	−0.15
Standard error		(0.51)	(0.56)		(0.52)	(0.55)
p-value		0.92	0.86		0.89	0.78
Female		−0.12	−0.11		−1.09*	−1.09*
Standard error		(0.53)	(0.60)		(0.52)	(0.54)
p-value		0.82	0.85		0.04	0.04
Married		0.15	0.34		−0.34	−0.23
Standard error		(0.65)	(0.75)		(0.68)	(0.73)
p-value		0.82	0.65		0.62	0.76
Household size: two people		0.19	0.31		−0.93	−0.93
Standard error		(0.79)	(0.88)		(0.82)	(0.85)
p-value		0.81	0.72		0.26	0.28
three or more		−0.30	0.02		−0.38	−0.24
Standard error		(0.70)	(0.81)		(0.78)	(0.82)
p-value		0.66	0.98		0.63	0.77
Education: high school diploma		−0.63	−0.61		−0.71	−0.71
Standard error		(0.79)	(0.89)		(0.63)	(0.64)
p-value		0.42	0.50		0.26	0.27
BA or more		−0.30	−0.41		−0.83	−1.19
Standard error		(0.81)	(0.96)		(0.70)	(0.76)
p-value		0.71	0.67		0.24	−.12
10+ years of work		0.76	0.83		1.21*	1.12+
Standard error		(0.56)	(0.67)		(0.61)	(0.63)
p-value		0.17	0.21		0.05	0.07
Good English		−0.33	−0.43		0.67	0.53
Standard error		(0.56)	(0.61)		(0.57)	(0.59)
p-value		0.56	0.48		0.24	0.37
Citizen		−0.33	−0.50		−0.75	−0.82
Standard error		(0.59)	(0.65)		(0.62)	(0.65)
p-value		0.59	0.45		0.23	0.21
Financial knowledge			0.08			0.04
Standard error			(0.22)			(0.21)
p-value			0.72			0.84
Program knowledge			0.22			0.27
Standard error			(0.21)			(0.21)
p-value			0.29			0.20
Tracking spending			0.07			0.12
Standard error			(0.40)			(0.42)
p-value			0.86			0.78
Ease w/bank staff			2.13*			0.48
Standard error			(0.88)			(1.21)
p-value			0.02			0.70
Constant	1.91*	2.27*	−0.17	−1.68**	−0.28	−1.43
Standard error	(0.54)	(1.15)	(1.51)	(0.39)	(0.94)	(1.61)
p-value	0.00	0.05	0.91	0.00	0.77	0.37

+p < 0.1; *p < 0.05; **p < 0.01

Table 3. Logit regression on financial outcomes.

	Banked			Long-term savings			Credit card			Retirement confidence		
	Model 1	Model 2	Model 3	Model 1	Model 2	Model 3	Model 1	Model 2	Model 3	Model 1	Model 2	Model 3
Korean	−1.80**	−2.08**	−2.16**	−1.34**	−1.59**	−1.72**	−0.47	−0.79+	−0.81+	0.37	0.32	0.56
Standard error	(0.66)	(0.71)	(0.76)	(0.41)	(0.46)	(0.50)	(0.39)	(0.43)	(0.48)	(0.54)	(0.58)	(0.63)
p-value	0.00	0.00	0.00	0.00	0.00	0.00	0.22	0.07	0.09	0.49	0.59	0.37
"Other Asian"	−1.73*	−2.24**	−2.11*	−1.02*	−1.18*	−1.06+	−0.25	−0.73	−0.91	1.30*	1.10+	1.23+
Standard error	(0.68)	(0.79)	(0.84)	(0.43)	(0.53)	(0.56)	(0.41)	(0.51)	(0.56)	(0.55)	(0.64)	(0.69)
p-value	0.01	0.01	0.01	0.02	0.03	0.06	0.55	0.15	0.10	0.02	0.09	0.08
Financial knowledge			0.12			0.03			0.14			−0.11
Standard error			(0.22)			(0.17)			(0.17)			(0.19)
p-value			0.59			0.86			0.39			0.55
Program knowledge			0.35+			0.11			0.01			0.29
Standard error			(0.2?)			(0.16)			(0.15)			(0.21)
p-value			0.10			0.50			0.97			0.18
Tracking spending			−0.10			−0.07			0.78**			0.41
Standard error			(0.45)			(0.30)			(0.29)			(0.36)
p-value			0.82			0.80			0.01			0.25
Ease w/bank staff			0.4?			1.82+			0.62			−0.25
Standard error			(1.1?)			(0.99)			(0.71)			(0.84)
p-value			0.7?			0.07			0.38			0.77

−p < 0.1; *p < 0.05; **p < 0.01

In addition to those variables reported in the table, Models 2 and 3 included age, gender, marital status, household size, education, work experience, English proficiency, and citizenship status.

Table 2 indicates that the three ethnic groups did not differ in likelihood of saving regularly (columns 4 to 6). In all three models, the ethnicity variables were not significant for asset accumulation. Moreover, none of the financial capability variables was statistically significant in the analyses of asset accumulation.

Table 3 reports logit regression results for the four other financial outcomes: ownership of a bank account, long-term savings, and credit card, and retirement confidence. To save space, Table 3 does not report on results of demographic, human capital, and citizenship status. Results on these variables were as expected. For example, English proficiency was positively associated with bank account ownership, credit card ownership, and retirement confidence. (Full analysis results are available from the authors.)

The first three columns in Table 3 show that Chinese respondents were significantly more likely to have a bank account than the other two ethnic group respondents. The coefficient sizes of ethnicity dummy variables were larger in Models 2 and 3 than those in Model 1, suggesting that ethnic differences in bank ownership were larger when demographic, human capital, citizenship, and financial capability were taken into account. It is noticeable that social program knowledge had a significantly positive association with bank account ownership. Results for long-term savings showed a similar pattern to those for bank account ownership. Koreans and "Other Asians" were less likely to have long-term savings, and controlling for demographic, human capital, citizenship, and financial capability did not reduce ethnic differences in long-term savings ownership. Among financial capability variables, ease in speaking with bank staff members was significantly and positively associated with one's chance of having long-term savings.

In terms of credit card ownership, Model 1 showed no significant differences by ethnicity. In Models 2 and 3, the coefficient of the Korean dummy variable was significantly negative at the 0.1 level, suggesting that Koreans were less likely to have a credit card than Chinese respondents with comparable characteristics. As shown in Table 1, Korean respondents were more likely to speak English proficiently than Chinese respondents, but the former were less likely to have a credit card than the latter. These facts may explain why a difference in credit card ownership between the two groups became statistically significant after controlling for English proficiency. Although not statistically significant at the 0.1 level ($p = 0.104$), the "Other Asian" variable had a large coefficient in Model 3. Financial management measured with tracking spending had a significant association with credit card ownership. The last three columns in Table 3 report results on retirement confidence. All three models indicated that "Other Asian" respondents were more likely to be confident in meeting basic expenses after retirement than Chinese respondents.

Discussion

We investigated various financial outcomes among low-income older Asian immigrants, using survey data collected from a subsided employment program in LA, OC, and NYC. We focused on ethnic differences and tested whether financial capability explains ethnic differences in various types of financial outcomes. According to the theoretical framework of financial capability, financial literacy and financial access are the main determinants of financial outcomes. Thus, it is plausible that ethnic differences in financial capability may contribute to ethnic disparities in financial outcomes among low-income older Asian immigrants.

Analysis results demonstrate the insecure financial conditions of low-income older Asian immigrants. Although the majority of respondents answered that they felt comfortable in opening a bank account and reported having a bank account, only 10% to 20% of respondents regularly saved, the majority did not have a credit card, and only 16% to 41% were confident about meeting basic expenses after retirement. These findings are not consistent with the popular image of economically successful Asian immigrants (Bascara, 2008).

Regression results indicate that ethnic differences in financial outcomes are not explained with differences in financial capability. For most financial outcome measures (having a bank account, long-term savings, and a credit card, and retirement confidence), ethnicity dummy variables did not lose statistical significance after controlling for demographics, human capital, citizenship, and financial capability. The coefficient sizes for ethnicity dummy variables were even larger in Models 2 and 3 than those in Model 1 for the ownership of a bank account, long-term savings, and a credit card, suggesting that ethnic differences become larger when these factors are taken into account. These findings do not support one of this study's hypotheses that ethnic disparities in financial outcomes may be caused by financial capability. However, these findings are not surprising if we consider bivariate analysis results. Korean respondents' financial outcomes were worse off than the other two groups despite their advantages in educational attainment, work experience in the United States, financial knowledge, and financial access. It seems, however, injudicious to make a conclusion solely based on the findings of this study. This study relies mainly on existing measures of financial literacy and access that were developed for the general population of the United States and did not pay attention to the unique financial experiences and environments of Asian immigrants. The use of imperfect measures may have resulted in a failure to capture the role of financial capability in explaining ethnic differences in financial outcomes. Thus, findings from this exploratory study may suggest the inadequacy of existing measures of financial capability in studying older Asian immigrants. In addition, as there are no other existing empirical studies on ethnic differences in financial capability and outcomes among older Asian immigrants, further theoretical discussion and empirical studies should be done before a conclusion on this issue can be reached.

Analysis results, however, back another hypothesis: Financial capability is associated with financial outcomes. Financial access was significantly and positively associated with chances of feeling comfortable in opening a bank account and of owning long-term savings accounts. Knowledge of social programs had a positive relationship with bank account ownership; financial management was positively associated with credit card ownership. To our best knowledge, this is the first study providing empirical evidence for the role of financial capability on financial outcomes among older Asian immigrants.

This study has limitations. One limitation is that we used data from a convenience sample consisting of NAPCA's SCSCEP participants in three locations. The sample may not be representative of all low-income older Asian immigrants in two ways. First, as active participants of a subsidized employment program that encourages the use of direct deposit services, the respondents in this study were likely better served by community organizations and had more opportunity to learn about financial services than individuals who may be isolated from ethnic communities. Second, the three locations of data collection had high percentages of Asian immigrants, and older Asian immigrants in areas with few Asians may have worse financial outcomes than those reported in this study. The second limitation of this study is that it used weak measures of financial access (ease in speaking with bank staff members) and financial outcomes. Although these measures assessed a certain aspect of financial access and financial outcomes respectively, this study was unable to capture other aspects of financial access (e.g., monetary burdens of financial services) and asset ownership (e.g., continuous measure of net worth). We decided not to collect information about dollar amount of each type of assets and debts needed in creating a continuous measure of net worth because of the risk of low item-response rates and time limitations. For example, item-response rates for dollar amount questions for nonsalient assets and liabilities range from 70% and 85% in the Survey of Consumer Finances, which used in-person interviews by trained interviewers (Fries, Starr-McCluer, & Sundén, 1998). Item-response rates would have been much lower in this study because we relied on a self-administered group survey. Including these questions would have increased survey time considerably. The third limitation is that cross-sectional survey data used in this study are limited in establishing causality. We cannot rule out the possibility that analyses in this study may have generated biased results due to unobserved variables. The fourth limitation is that this study shows that ethnic disparities in financial outcomes exist, but cannot explain why these groups differed from each other. In sum, although this study expands our understanding of financial capability and financial outcomes, it leaves many questions unanswered.

Findings in this exploratory study have the following implications for future research and practices. Further investigation is warranted to explain ethnic disparities in financial outcomes in this population. For example, future research may examine the roles of (extended) family's economic networks (e.g., economic resource pooling); outreach efforts toward immigrants among financial institutions, especially among ethnic banks; community support systems; and informal financial institutions (e.g., rotating saving and credit associations) in explaining group differences in wealth and financial outcomes. In addition, findings of this study call for the development of more reliable and valid measures of financial capability for Asian immigrants. This study relies mainly on existing measures of financial literacy and access because of the lack of culturally suitable measures. New valid and reliable financial capability measures developed for this population will expand our understanding of older Asian immigrants' economic security and prospects.

This study's findings call for active roles among social workers and community organizers in advocating for older Asian immigrants' long-term economic security. As shown in this study, this population is financially insecure. Accordingly, social workers and community organizers should educate policy makers and the general public about the myth of the model minority while calling for active policy interventions to enhance long-term economic security among this population. For example, social workers and community organizers should organize themselves and other interested groups in policy advocacy to expand financial access among low-income older Asian Americans (e.g., bilingual financial services and culturally-suitable financial products). As frontline service providers, social workers and community organizers should be equipped with financial knowledge to provide financial education and planning services for their clients and develop culturally-suitable and age-appropriate financial programs. Furthermore, social workers and community organizers should be aware that older Asian immigrants are heterogeneous. Accordingly, they should be aware of unique financial conditions and cultural values among various Asian groups and develop culturally suitable services and policies to meet various needs in older Asian immigrants.

Acknowledgments

This study was supported in part by grants from the Les Brun Research Endowment Fund at University at Buffalo, and the Civic Engagement Research Dissemination Fellowship Program at University at Buffalo. We are thankful to Christine Takada, Miriam Suen, Helen Jang, Norman Lee, Junghee Han, Xiao Yu Yang, Kerry Situ, and Yong-Jin Ahn for their assistance with data collection. We are grateful to Ya-Ling Chen, Junpyo Kim, Amanda Brower, and Sarah Nesbitt for their research assistance. This study was approved by the Social and Behavioral Science Institutional Review Board of the University at Buffalo (Study #4759).

References

Asian Americans Advancing Justice. (2011). *A community of contrasts: Asian Americans in the United States, 2011*. Washington, DC: Author.

Bascara, V. (2008). Model minority. In R. T. Schaefer (Ed.), *Encyclopedia of race, ethnicity, and society* (pp. 910–912). Thousand Oaks, CA: Sage.

Behrman, J. R., Mitchell, O. S., Soo, C., & Bravo, D. (2010). *Financial literacy, schooling, and wealth accumulation*. Cambridge, MA: National Bureau of Economic Research.

Beverly, S. G. (2006). *Financial knowledge, attitudes, ownership, and practices among families in the SEED pre-school demonstration and impact assessment*. Lawrence, KS: University of Kansas, School of Social Welfare.

Borjas, G. J. (2002). Homeownership in the immigrant population. *Journal of Urban Economics, 52*, 448–476. doi:10.1016/S0094-1190(02)00529-6

Chang, M. L. (2012). *Shortchanged: Why women have less wealth and what can be done about it*. New York, NY: Oxford University Press.

Cobb-Clark, D. A., & Hildebrand, V. A. (2006). The wealth and asset holdings of US-born and foreign-born households: Evidence from SIPP data. *Review of Income and Wealth, 52*, 17–42. doi:10.1111/roiw.2006.52.issue-1

Congressional Budget Office. (2004). *A description of the immigrant population*. Washington, DC: Congress of the United States.

Denton, M., & Boos, L. (2007). The gender wealth gap: Structural and material constraints and implications for later life. *Journal of Women & Aging, 19*, 105–120. doi:10.1300/J074v19n03_08

Employee Benefit Research Institute. (2003). *The 2003 minority retirement confidence survey summary of findings*. Issue Brief. Washington, DC: Employee Benefit Research Institute.

Federal Interagency Forum on Aging-Related Statistics. (2012). *Older Americans 2012: Key indicators of well-being*. Washington, DC: US Government Printing Office.

Fries, G., Starr-McCluer, M., & Sundén, A. E. (1998). *The measurement of household wealth using survey data: An overview of the Survey of Consumer Finances*. Washington, DC: Federal Reserve Board of Governors.

Gould, E., & Cooper, D. (2013). *Financial security of elderly Americans at risk*. Washington, DC: Economic Policy Institute.

Hao, L. (2007). *Color lines, country lines: Race, immigration, and wealth stratification in America*. New York, NY: Russell Sage Foundation.

He, W., Sengupta, M., Velkoff, V. A., & DeBarros, K. A. (2005). *65+ in the United States: 2005*. Washington, DC: US Census Bureau.

Huang, J., Nam, Y., & Sherraden, M. S. (2013). Financial knowledge and child development account policy: A test of financial capability. *Journal of Consumer Affairs, 47*, 1–26.

Hurh, W. M., & Kim, K. C. (1989). The 'success' image of Asian Americans: Its validity, and its practical and theoretical implications. *Ethnic and Racial Studies, 12*, 512–538. doi:10.1080/01419870.1989.9993650

Li, W. (2014). Asian Ethnic banks. In X. Zhao & E. J. W. Park (Eds.), *Asian Americans: An Encyclopedia of Social, Cultural, and Political History*. Santa Barbara, California: Greenwood.

Little, R. J. A., & Rubin, D. B. (2002). *Statistical analysis with missing data* (2nd ed.). Hoboken, NJ: John Wiley & Sons.

Lusardi, A., & Mitchell, O. S. (2007). Financial literacy and retirement preparedness: Evidence and implications for financial education. *Business Economics, 42,* 35–44. doi:10.2145/20070104

Lusardi, A., & Tufano, P. (2009). *Debt literacy, financial experiences, and overindebtedness* (NBER Working Paper No. 14808). Cambridge, MA: National Bureau of Economic Research.

Moya, J. C. (2005). Immigrants and associations: A global and historical perspective. *Journal of Ethnic and Migration Studies, 31,* 833–864. doi:10.1080/13691830500178147

Nam, Y. (2014). Immigration and economic conditions among older Asian Americans. *Race and Social Problems, 6,* 15–24. doi:10.1007/s12552-014-9118-1

Nam, Y. (2015). Older immigrants: Economic security, asset ownership, financial access, and public policy. In M. S. Sherraden, & N. Morrow-Howell (Eds.), *Financial capability and asset holding in later life: A life course perspective* (pp. 104–119). New York, NY: Oxford University Press.

Nam, Y., Lee, E. J., Huang, J., & Kim, J. (2015). Financial capability and asset ownership among low-income older Asian immigrants. *Journal of Gerontological Social Work, 58,* 114–127. doi:10.1080/01634372.2014.923085

National Asian Pacific Center on Aging. (2013). *Asian American and Pacific Islanders in the United States aged 55 years and older: Population, nativity, and language.* Seattle, WA: National Asian Pacific Center on Aging.

Osili, U. O., & Paulson, A. (2008). Institutions and financial development: Evidence from international migrants in the United States. *Review of Economics and Statistics, 90*(3), 498–517.

Sakamoto, A., Goyette, K. A., & Kim, C. H. (2009). Socioeconomic attainments of Asian Americans. *Annual Review of Sociology, 35,* 255–276. doi:10.1146/annurev-soc-070308-115958

Schafer, J. L., & Graham, J. W. (2002). Missing data: Our view of the state of the art. *Psychological Methods, 7,* 147–177. doi:10.1037/1082-989X.7.2.147

Sevak, P., & Schmidt, L. (2007, October). *How do immigrants fare in retirement?* (Working Paper 2007-169). Ann Arbor, MI: Michigan Retirement Research Center, University of Michigan.

Shanks, T. R. W., & Leigh, W. A. (2015). Assets and older African Americans. In M. S. Sherraden, & N. Morrow-Howell (Eds.), *Financial capability and asset holding in later life: A life course perspective* (pp. 49–68). New York, NY: Oxford University Press.

Sherraden, M. S. (2013). Building blocks of financial capability. In J. Birkenmaier, M. Sherraden, & J. Curley (Eds.), *Financial capability and asset development: Research, education, policy, and practice* (pp. 3–43). New York, NY: Oxford University Press.

STATACorp. (2009). *STATA multiple imputation reference manual, release 11.* College Station, TX: StataCorp LP.

Taylor, P., Kochhar, R., Fry, R., Velasco, G., & Motel, S. (2011). Twenty-to-one: Wealth gaps rise to record highs between Whites, Blacks and Hispanics. *Pew Social & Demographic Trends.* Washington, DC: Pew Research Center.

US Census Bureau. (2015). *Annual estimates of the resident population by sex, age, race, and Hispanic Origin for the United States and States: April 1, 2010 to July 1, 2014.* Washington, DC: U.S. Census Bureau, Population Division.

US Department of Treasury. (2010). Financial education core competencies. *Federal Register, 75,* 52596–52597.

Financial Knowledge and Behaviors of Chinese Migrant Workers: An International Perspective on a Financially Vulnerable Population

Zibei Chen and Catherine M. Lemieux

ABSTRACT

Making informed financial decisions is crucial to the wellbeing of Chinese migrant workers. Using interview survey data ($N = 329$), this study examined financial knowledge and behaviors of migrant workers in China. Results showed that participants demonstrated low levels of financial knowledge (51.4%) and beneficial financial behaviors (51.0%). Multivariate results indicated that a modest proportion of the variance in financial behaviors was explained by financial knowledge, attitudes, and socio-demographic characteristics (e.g., marital status and income). Findings underscore the importance of disseminating culturally-relevant educational interventions to financially at-risk, low-paid migrant workers in China.

Over the past 2 decades in China, an estimated 262 million individuals migrated from rural areas to cities for job opportunities (National Bureau Statistics of China [NBSC], 2012), a substantial population of workers that plays a critical role in China's rapid economic development. This unprecedented and extensive rural-to-urban migration has provided migrant workers with new opportunities to increase their household income and financial wellbeing, but it also has rendered them as one of the most socially and economically disadvantaged groups in China (Song & Appleton, 2008; Wong, Fu, Li, & Song, 2007). Lu (2008) noted that a major contributor to migrant workers' disadvantaged status is China's institutionalized household registration system (viz., *hukou*), a social control policy that has disenfranchised rural migrant workers and their families, preventing them from legitimately gaining long-term urban residency and access to stable employment, affordable housing, and social security, benefits that are available to Chinese urban residents (Chen, Lucas, Bloom, & Ding, 2010; Ngok, 2012). Further, when social welfare programs are made available to Chinese migrant workers, research shows that only a small proportion actually participates

(Cheng, Nielsen, & Smyth, 2014; Song & Appleton, 2008; Xu, Guan, & Yao, 2011). Given that migrant workers represent some of the least educated and lowest paid workers in China (Wong et al., 2007), they are especially vulnerable to financial emergencies and economic instability (Wong et al., 2007; Song & Appleton, 2008). With few social policies in place to protect Chinese migrant workers' economic wellbeing (Chen et al., 2010), having the requisite financial knowledge and skills to make informed financial decisions is of paramount importance.

As China implements ongoing social and economic reforms, rural-to-urban Chinese migrants continue to be denied access to residency-based welfare benefits and public services (Chen et al., 2010). Without benefits or insurance, migrant workers employed in the less-skilled industry sectors are especially vulnerable to economic uncertainties, such as health emergencies or job loss (Song & Appleton, 2008). Thus, the ability to make informed financial decisions is important to migrant workers' financial stability and wellbeing. However, little is known about the financial literacy (i.e., financial knowledge and skills) of Chinese migrant workers. To address this gap in the literature, this study examined financial literacy and decision making of migrant workers employed in an urban setting. This exploratory-descriptive study sought to develop a preliminary understanding of Chinese migrant workers' financial lives, with particular emphasis on how they perceive and manage their finances in an unfavorable socio-economic environment.

Background of study

Financial literacy: definition and measurement

Financial literacy is a concept that has received heightened scholarly interest since the 1990s and has been defined in various ways in the research. Some studies have narrowly defined financial literacy as the understanding of basic financial concepts and key financial terms (Bowen, 2002; Lusardi & Mitchell, 2011; National Council on Economic Education, 2005); others conceptualized financial literacy as the ability to use the knowledge to make informed financial decisions (Beal & Delpachitra, 2003; Jump$tart Coalition for Personal Financial Literacy, 2007; Mandell, 2006). A number of scholars have argued that other aspects, such as financial practical experience, self-efficacy, and attitudes, are important components because research has linked these latter concepts to financial literacy and behaviors across different populations of consumers (Caratelli & Ricci, 2011; Danes & Haberman; 2004; Moore, 2003). More often, however, financial literacy has not been explicitly conceptualized in the extant research, and readers have had to infer the definition from how researchers measured the construct (Chen & Volpe, 2002; Servon & Kaestner, 2008). After analyzing over 100 studies, a number of scholars in the field (viz., Hung, Parker, & Yoong, 2009; Remund, 2010) concluded that financial literacy is a multidimensional concept that warrants a composite definition.

Given the definitional ambiguity of the term, there is little consensus regarding how financial literacy should be operationalized. The research to date has been highly contextualized, and studies have measured financial literacy using different instruments in which the content, number of items, and types of questions have varied considerably. For example, researchers have not only examined knowledge of basic financial concepts, budgeting, saving, borrowing, and investment (Goldsmith & Goldsmith, 2006; Lusardi, 2008; Perry & Morris, 2005), but also confidence, attitudes, and personal experience concerning money management (Danes & Haberman, 2004; Lyons, Chang, & Scherpf, 2006; Moore, 2003). Questionnaire items for existing surveys typically have taken the form of true-false (Financial Industry Regulatory Authority, 2003) or multiple-choice questions (Chen & Volpe, 1998), or a combination of both (Lusardi & Mitchell, 2008; Zhan, Anderson, & Scott, 2006). Instruments used to assess financial literacy have ranged from 5 (Chang & Lyons, 2007) to over 100 items (Kempson, Collard, Turtle, & Worley, 2006). Thus, there is tremendous variability in how financial literacy has been assessed and measured across studies. However, knowledge of and skills with budgeting, saving, borrowing, and investing are universally considered essential to effective money management and are frequently measured in previous studies of financial literacy (e.g., Hung et al., 2009; Huston, 2010).

Prevalence of low levels of financial literacy

Despite the variability in how financial literacy has been measured, the findings of studies conducted worldwide generally converge, indicating that levels of financial knowledge are quite low in developed countries such as the United States (Hogarth & Hilgert, 2002), the United Kingdom (Atkinson, McKay, Kempson, & Collard, 2006), Australia (Worthington, 2006), Japan (Organization for Economic Co-operation Development [OECD], 2005), and the Netherlands (Van Rooij, Lusardi, & Alessie, 2011). For example, American adults correctly answered approximately two-thirds of question-naire items assessing financial literacy (Hogarth & Hilgert, 2002); whereas respondents in Germany were able to correctly answer only half of the relevant questions about financial knowledge (OECD, 2005). Current research shows that financial knowledge is especially low among certain populations. In the United States, for example, Huston (2010) reviewed over 71 studies and concluded that financial literacy levels are especially low among older American adults (Chang & Lyons, 2007; Lusardi & Mitchell, 2007), high school and college students (Kindle, 2010; Loke & Hageman, 2013), and low-income populations (Zhan et al., 2006). Huston

(2010) observed that educational attainment and income are consistently and positively associated with financial literacy.

However, these latter findings should be interpreted with caution because of methodological and other issues. For example, Huston (2010) observed that studies do not always provide a clear definition of the construct, financial literacy. There are related issues with measurement. The reliability of instruments used to assess financial literacy is questionable, with the majority of studies using subjective measures such as perceived knowledge (e.g., Lyons et al., 2006) and self-report behaviors (e.g., Zhan et al., 2006). In addition, studies often focus on only one or two aspects of financial literacy, largely ignoring the multidimensional nature of financial knowledge and behaviors (Hung et al., 2009). Representativeness is also an issue, in that respondents frequently are self-selected, thereby limiting the generalizability of the findings to individuals willing to disclose their money-management activities (e.g., Zhan et al., 2006).

Little research has been undertaken in developing countries; however, levels of financial literacy in countries such as India and Indonesia are especially low (Xu & Zia, 2013). No study, to date, has examined the financial knowledge and behaviors of Chinese migrant workers.

Financial behaviors

Although often considered one aspect of financial literacy in the extant research (see, e.g., Remund, 2010), financial behaviors are defined as specific actions pertaining to money management undertaken by consumers (Xiao, 2008). Examples of positive financial behaviors include using credit cards responsibly (Allgood & Walstad, 2011), saving for emergencies (Babiarz & Robb, 2014), and engaging in other desirable money-management activities such as budgeting and low-cost borrowing (Kempson et al., 2006; Lusardi & Mitchell, 2008; Lyons et al., 2006). Conversely, Garman and colleagues observed that poor financial behaviors consist of a pattern of practices that negatively impacts an individual's life at home and in the workplace (Garman & Forgue, 2014). More than the common financial mistakes occasionally made by most working individuals at some point (e.g., overspending, overusing credit, running out of money; writing checks without sufficient funds, having no emergency or retirement savings), poor financial behaviors are financial errors that occur with regularity and that incur negative consequences, such as stress, anxiety, family conflict, and loss of assets (Garman, Leech, & Grable, 1997).

Studies of consumer money-management activities typically have focused on problematic financial behaviors and found inadequate levels of financial knowledge as one contributing factor. For example, Babiarz and Robb (2014) recently examined consumers' savings behaviors using a nationally-representative sample and found those with higher levels of financial knowledge were more likely to report having emergency funds. Lusardi (2013) similarly found a strong correlation between financial knowledge and behaviors: Individuals who were more financially literate were less likely to engage in high-cost borrowing activities. In addition, both of these latter studies on financial behavior showed interrelationships among income, education level, and financial behaviors; namely, the lower the income and education, the lower the likelihood of having savings and the greater the likelihood of engaging in high-cost borrowing (Babiarz & Robb, 2014; Lusardi, 2013).

Financial literacy and behaviors in China and among migrant workers

Very little research on financial literacy has been undertaken with Chinese populations, despite the economic changes that have taken place in that country in the last decade. Our search yielded three exploratory studies that focused on fairly circumscribed aspects of financial literacy. Song (2011) surveyed 1,104 rural household members about their knowledge of compound interest using a single survey item and found that fewer than one in five (18%) were able to correctly answer the question. In addition, a positive association emerged between knowledge of compound interest and the amounts contributed to pension plans (Song, 2011). Utilizing a national sample of 3,122 Chinese adults, Xia, Wang, and Li (2014) examined participants' knowledge of the stock market (i.e., investment risk, stocks and bonds, foreign exchange rate) with a 7-item survey and found that nearly half of respondents (42.9%) were either underconfident or overconfident about their knowledge and at risk of making unwise decisions with regard to stock market participation. Using a 3-item questionnaire, Yu, Wu, Chan, and Chou (2015) examined gender differences in financial knowledge among 1,005 Hong Kong workers and found that female respondents were less likely than their male counterparts to correctly respond to the items. Similar to the research undertaken in other countries (e.g., OECD, 2005), these latter exploratory studies of financial literacy (viz., Song, 2011; Xia et al., 2014; Yu et al., 2015) assessed participants' financial knowledge in very specific areas using brief, subjective, self-report measures that lacked demonstrated validity and reliability. In addition, none of the studies sampled migrant workers, a sizable subpopulation of low-paid workers in China.

Rural-to-urban migration has increased migrant workers' income levels (De Brauw & Giles, 2012; Taylor, Rozelle & De Brauw, 2003), but it also has exacerbated their economic vulnerability (Xu et al., 2011). Chinese migrant workers seem to have some awareness of their heightened risk, with studies showing fairly high rates of saving and remittance among this sub-population of workers (Chen, Lu, & Zhong, 2015; Giles & Yoo, 2007; Zhu, Wu, Wang, Du, & Cai, 2012). The research suggests that the saving behavior of Chinese migrant workers is precautionary and linked to their socio-economic status, circumstances characterized by unstable employment, low wages, and ineligibility for many institutionalized social benefits (Chen et al., 2015; Giles & Yoo, 2007). Research also showed that, because of high mobility and few investment opportunities, migrant workers tend to consume fewer durable goods and use funds to build houses in rural areas (Chen et al., 2015; De Brauw & Rozelle, 2008). In sum, research investigating the economic behaviors of Chinese migrant workers has utilized aggregate-level data to examine certain financial behaviors, such as patterns of saving, remittance, and consumption, but has not explored migrant workers' financial knowledge and behaviors in a systematical manner.

Summary and implications of literature review

Methodological limitations notwithstanding, the corpus of research on financial literacy undertaken in the last 2 decades points to a positive association between financial knowledge and responsible financial behaviors (see, e.g., Babiarz & Robb, 2014; Hilgert, Hogarth, & Beverly, 2003), with studies across diverse samples worldwide underscoring the importance of financial literacy to overall economic wellbeing (OECD, 2005; Xu & Zia, 2013). Of particular concern to social work is the economic wellbeing of low-income and other economically vulnerable populations (Birkenmaier & Curley, 2009; Zhan et al., 2006). Rural-to-urban migrant workers, who comprise a substantial portion of the Chinese workforce and have played a critical role in China's economic development, represent one such group. The marginalized socioeconomic status of rural-to-urban migrant workers renders them especially vulnerable to economic instability (Wong et al., 2007). In fact, the economic wellbeing of disenfranchised Chinese migrant workers has garnered the attention of researchers and policymakers since the rural-to-urban migration took place in China in the mid-1990s. Although surveys of financial knowledge have been undertaken with rural Chinese populations (e.g., Yu et al., 2015), there is a dearth of research examining the financial literacy of Chinese rural migrant workers.

Given that migrant workers typically become financially independent at a young age (NBSC, 2012), their long-term economic stability is contingent upon their ability to make sound financial decisions over time. Further, within the context of China's ongoing rural-to-urban migration and concomitant socioeconomic reforms (Chen et al., 2010), knowledge about the financial knowledge and behaviors of migrant workers is especially timely (Ngok, 2012; Song & Appleton, 2008). The current cross-sectional, descriptive study is the first known study to examine the financial knowledge and behaviors of Chinese rural-to-urban migrant workers. Effective money management is the cornerstone of financial literacy (OECD, 2005; Remund, 2010); thus, as recommended by researchers and policymakers in the field (see, e.g., Hung et al., 2009; Volpe, Chen, & Liu, 2006; Zhan et al., 2006), this study specifically focused on four areas of financial literacy that are essential to effective money management: knowledge about budgeting, saving, borrowing, and investing. The following research questions framed this study:

(1) What is the level of financial literacy (i.e., knowledge about money management) among Chinese rural migrant workers?
(2) Does level of financial knowledge differ with respect to workers' income, education level, and length of employment?
(3) What are the primary sources of financial knowledge reported by Chinese migrant workers?
(4) To what extent do Chinese migrant workers engage in beneficial financial behaviors?
(5) What combination of relevant correlates (viz., financial knowledge, attitude toward finances, socio-demographic characteristics) best predicts workers' beneficial financial behaviors?

Method

Study design and procedure

This exploratory-descriptive study sampled migrant workers employed at a Chinese university located in Beijing, the capital city of China, in July of 2010. There were two reasons for using a large, urban university as the study site. First, a member of the research team was a graduate student at this particular university, and therefore had relatively access to the population of migrant workers on campus. Second, Chinese universities in the larger cities have a variety of unskilled, low-wage jobs in the catering and service industries that are predominately filled by migrant workers. Given the paucity of research examining the financial knowledge and behaviors of Chinese migrant workers, the use of an availability sample is appropriate, given the exploratory nature of the current study.

This cross-sectional study used a convenience sampling method with employment sector as the sampling element. A nonprobability sampling approach was appropriate because migrant workers demonstrate high rates of mobility and do not register as residents (Landry & Shen, 2005); thus it is not possible to employ a probability sampling method with this population. Further, according to the NBSC (2012), migrant workers employed in the same sector are fairly homogenous in terms of their demographic characteristics. For example, the construction field employs more male workers, whereas the service industry employs younger migrant workers (NBSC, 2012). To collect a relatively heterogeneous sample, this study purposefully recruited prospective participants from different employment sectors available on campus. The content herein provides a detailed description of the procedures used to recruit participants.

A member of the research team consulted with a representative from the university personnel office to obtain information about the migrant workers employed on campus. The researchers identified a total of approximately 1,300 rural migrant workers who held jobs in six employment sectors, most of whom were from rural areas in central and northeastern China. Although it was not possible to determine the exact number of eligible participants, the researcher was able to identify the approximate proportion of migrant workers employed in each of the six sectors (see Table 1). The researcher then made multiple visits to the workplaces of prospective study participants, asking them to participate in the current study. Once verbal consent was obtained, the researcher administered a survey packet consisting of the consent letter and survey instrument. All migrant workers were informed that their participation was voluntary and anonymous. The researcher conducted face-to-face interviews with participants and offered a small incentive (facial towels) for their participation in the research. Only 2 of the 331 workers who were approached by the researcher refused to participate. Thus, the total sample consisted of 329 migrant workers who provided consent and completed individual interviews with the researcher.

As seen in Table 1, the sample obtained for this study was proportionally representative of the population of migrant workers in each employment sector on campus. This was confirmed by the personnel officer at the university from which the sample was drawn. Further, national-level data suggest that migrant workers sampled in the current study were working in industries (i.e., catering, construction, service) that are not dissimilar to those employing large numbers of workers throughout China. According to the recent national report, the majority of Chinese migrant workers were employed in the manufacturing and construction industries (at 35.7% and 18.4%, respectively); followed by the accommodation, catering, and service sectors, which employed approximately 45.5 million

Table 1. Summary of the distribution of participants by employment sector.

Employment Sector	No. Response	%	% of Migrant Workers on Campus
Catering Department	113	34.35	40
Logistic Department (Cleaning and Security)	60	18.24	20
Communication and Service (Hotels & Restaurants)	48	14.59	12
Dormitory Management	19	5.78	5
Business Center (Retails & Student Services)	35	10.64	10
Construction	54	16.41	13
Total	329	100	100

(17.4%) migrant workers (NBSC, 2012). It must be emphasized, however, that disaggregated national-level data are needed to more accurately determine to what extent on-campus migrant workers differ from those employed in different settings. This study was approved by the Human Subjects Review committee of the researcher's affiliated university.

Participants

Table 2 provides a summary of socio-demographic information of the sample. The sample (N = 329) was primarily composed of single (61.7%), male (57.5%) migrant workers who were, on average, 26 years of age (SD = 8.0). Among those who were married (n = 126), the vast majority had dependent children (n = 120, 94.4%). More than half (56.34%) of respondents did not complete high school education. The average monthly wage was $243 ($SD$ = $104; US $1 ≈ 6.78 Chinese yuan, as of July 2010). Participants reported that they had been employed, on average, for 7.5 years (SD = 5.8). Over half (57.1%) had been employed for 5 or more years.

Measurement

The instrument used in this current study was the Basic Financial Literacy Survey (BFLS), a researcher-developed tool that collected data about participants' financial literacy and relevant socio-demographic information. The BFLS is composed of a financial knowledge test (23 items) and scales that assess financial behaviors

Table 2. Sample characteristics (N = 329).

	n	percent
Gender		
Male	189	57.45%
Female	140	42.55%
Marital Status		
Single	203	61.7%
Married	126	38.3%
Children		
Yes	120	36.59%
No	128	63.41%
Education		
Primary school	14	4.26%
Middle school	171	51.98%
High school	97	29.48%
Vocational school	42	12.77%
College	5	1.52%
	Mean	SD
Age	26	8
Monthly Income	$243 (¥ 1652)	$104 (¥ 705)
Years of Employment	7.5	5.8

(5 items), attitudes toward money management (1 item), and sources of financial knowledge (3 items), as well as a section that collects socio-demographic information (8 items). Items measuring financial knowledge and financial behaviors were heavily drawn from various instruments used in previous studies (e.g., Lusardi & Mitchell, 2005; Moore, 2003; Vitt et al., 2000; Volpe, Chen, & Pavlicko, 1996; Worthington, 2006), and then translated to Chinese using culturally appropriate contextual modifications. Throughout the data collection process, the researcher used the BFLS to structure the interviews and recorded participants' responses to all questions on the BFLS tool.

The survey instrument was pretested with 8 migrant workers who were employed on campus in April and May of 2010 whose responses were not included in this study. As a result of the pretest, the researcher contextualized the content of some BFLS questions to be more relevant to migrant workers' financial lives. Due to concerns about the reading skills of prospective respondents, the wording of some items was simplified to ensure that the meaning was understandable to workers with limited formal education. Next, the modified version of the BFLS survey was assessed by two independent evaluators who were experts in personal finance and knowledgeable about the Chinese migrant worker population.[1] It should be noted that the wording of BFLS questions used in this study was relatively simpler than that used in previous studies of financial literacy among college students (Chen & Volpe, 2002) and workers in the U.S. (Lusardi & Mitchell, 2007).

Financial knowledge

The BFLS assessed three categories of financial knowledge, including basic arithmetic (5 items), saving and borrowing (11 items), and investment and risk (7 items). Questions about basic arithmetic were adapted from Worthington (2006); the remaining 18 items were adapted from Bernheim (1998), Chen and Volpe (1998), Lusardi and Mitchell (2005), and Moore (2003). As recommended by Chen and Volpe (2002), correct responses to questions in all categories were coded as 1 and incorrect responses were coded as 0. The total number of correct responses was summed. Total financial knowledge scale scores ranged from 0–23, with higher scores indicating higher levels of financial knowledge. The 23-item financial knowledge scale showed acceptable internal consistency (coefficient alpha = 0.76).

Basic arithmetic

Five questions asked respondents to complete operations of addition, subtraction, multiplication and division. For example, subtraction and multiplication skills were assessed with the question, *The price of a brand new*

---

[1] A copy of the survey instrument is available from the authors upon request.

television is ¥250. Shop A takes ¥30 off the price while shop B takes 10% off the price. Which shop offers lower price of this television? (The response, *Shop A*, is the correct answer and was coded 1, otherwise coded 0.) Total arithmetic subscale scores ranged from 0–5, with higher scores demonstrating higher levels of math skills.

Saving and borrowing

Eleven questions assessed participants' knowledge about savings interest (4 items), inflation (3 items), borrowing interest and related responsibilities (3 items) and ATM use (1 item). For example, knowledge about savings interest was assessed with a question, *Suppose you had ¥100 in a savings account and the fixed interest rate is 20% per year. After 5 years, how much would you have in this account in total?* Response options included *(i) ¥200, (ii) ¥500, (iii) more than ¥200, (iv) Do not know (DK).* (Answer *iii* was considered correct and coded as 1, the others were coded as 0.) Participants' knowledge about borrowing responsibilities was measured with an item, *Generally speaking, do you get any kind of penalty if you can't pay off the debt on time?* Response options included *(i) no penalty, (ii) probably have to pay more, (iii) yes, must pay fines, (iv) DK.* (Answer *iii* was considered correct and coded 1, otherwise 0.) Total saving and borrowing subscale scores ranged from 0–11, with higher scores indicating greater levels of saving and borrowing knowledge.

Investment and risk

To measure knowledge about investment and risk, participants were asked 7 questions. Two were about safe investments and the remaining five focused on (a) the relationship between risk and return, (b) risk diversification, (c) beneficial and safe-saving types of risk, (d) losing a debit card, and (e) participating in illegal financing. The item assessing knowledge about the relationship between risk and return, for example, asked participants to choose the correct statement among the following: *(i) high risk often brings low return, (ii) low risk often brings high return, (iii) high risk brings high return, (iv) DK.* (Answer *iii* was correct, and coded 1, other responses were coded 0.) The question and response options pertaining to knowledge about risk and diversification were worded as follows: *When an investor spreads his/her money among different assets, does the risk of losing money (i) increase, (ii) decrease, (iii) stay the same, (iv) DK.* (Answer *ii* was correct and coded 1, other response were coded 0.) Total investment and risk subscale scores ranged from 0–7, with higher scores indicating higher levels of investment knowledge.

Financial behaviors

The BFLS includes five multiple-choice questions assessing participants' self-reported financial behaviors in the areas of bookkeeping, budgeting, making ends meet, saving for retirement, and saving for emergency. Although the items assess self-reported rather than observed behaviors, these latter activities were considered important in previous studies (e.g., Hilgert et al., 2003), and these latter financial behaviors were assessed in large-scale surveys undertaken in other countries (e.g., *Survey of Consumer Finances* in the United States, *Survey of Adult Financial Literacy* in Australia). The responses were recoded as dichotomous variables to calculate scores. Respondents received a score of 1 if at least one favorable financial behavior was reported for each category. Financial behavior scores ranged from 0–5, with higher scores indicating higher levels of self-reported responsible financial behaviors.

Bookkeeping, budgeting, making ends meet

The question about bookkeeping was, *Do you keep track of money?* The response options included: *(i) no, I have no idea where my money goes, (ii) no, but I have a rough idea where money goes, (iii) I do sometimes, but still not sure where money goes, (iv) I do sometimes, and have a rough idea where my money goes, (v) I do keep a record of money and know exactly where my money goes.* (Answers *ii*, *iv*, and *v* were considered favorable behaviors in that all three convey an awareness of the importance of tracking money. These latter three responses were therefore coded as 1, and the other responses were coded 0.) The item about budgeting was worded: *Do you use a monthly budget?* Response options included: *(i) no, I don't, (ii) sometimes I do, but my spending does not align with budget; (iii) sometimes I do, and my spending sticks to the budget, (iv) I do, but my spending does not align with budget, (v) I do, and my spending always stick to budget.* (Using and following budget is considered a sound money-management practice, therefore, answers *iii* and *v* were coded as 1 and the other responses were coded as 0.) The question about making ends meet was worded as follows: *Are you living paycheck to paycheck each month?* The response options were: *(i) yes, I usually don't have money left at the end of each month, (ii) yes, and I usually live beyond my means, (iii) yes, but a few times I have a little money left, (iv) no, I have some money each month, (v) no, I have a planned amount of money left each month.* (Answers *iv* and *v* both indicate favorable saving behavior, and were coded as 1, other responses were coded as 0.)

Saving for emergencies and retirement

According to the National Financial Capability Study (2009), the minimum amount of time for which living expenses should be covered when saving for emergencies is 3 months. Participants were asked about their savings for emergencies with the following question: *How long would your emergency funds last, if any, if you became unemployed at this moment?* Six response options were provided, including: *(i) I would be in financial trouble immediately, (ii) a month, (iii) 3–5 months, (iv) a year, (v) longer than a year, (vi) DK.* (Although the response options were not mutually exclusive, answers *iii, iv*, and *v* were considered favorable answers and coded 1, other answers were coded 0.) The question about saving for retirement was worded, *Have you begun preparing for retirement?* Response options included: *(i) never thought about it, (ii) it occurred to me sometimes, but I have no idea how to prepare, (iii) I plan on depending on my children, (iv) I've considered and taken action.* Answer *iii* was included as a contextual modification that reflects China's patterns of intergenerational support for retirement. As recommended by Lusardi and Mitchell (2005), those who chose answer *iv* were considered committed planners; thus, response *iv* was coded as 1, others were coded as 0.

Attitude, source of financial knowledge

Attitude toward finances was assessed with one item that asked participants to choose the statement that best reflected their attitude toward money management: *(i) money management matters only when you have a large amount of money, (ii) money management matters only when you have very little money, (iii) money management matters no matter how much money you have, (iv) making money is so much more important that money management can be ignored.* Money management is necessary regardless of one's financial situation, therefore answer *iii* was considered the favorable attitude toward money management and coded 1, and other responses were coded 0. Three separate questions asked respondents about their source of financial knowledge (viz., primary, most beneficial, and most reliable). The following six options were provided for each item: *(i) magazines, books, television and radio stations; (ii) formal financial organizations; (iii) school education; (iv) family, friend, and coworkers; (v) internet; (vi) trial and error.*

Data analysis

Univariate statistics were used to summarize data about financial knowledge, behaviors, attitudes, sources of financial knowledge, and socio-demographic information. Socio-demographic variables were dichotomized prior to bivariate analyses, including age (0 = *23 years old or younger*, 1 = *24 years old or older*), gender (0 = *female*, 1 = *male*), marital status (0 = *single*, 1 = *married*), dependent child (0 = *no child*, 1 = *have dependent child*), educational attainment (0 = *less than high school*, 1 = *high school and above*), monthly income (0 = *less than $243*, 1 = *$243 or more*), years of employment (0 = *5 years or* *less*, 1 = *more than 5 years*), and attitude toward finances (0 = *unfavorable*, 1 = *favorable*). The median value was used to determine the cut-off point for dichotomizing all sociodemographic variables. Independent *t*-tests were computed to examine differences in level of financial knowledge across socio-demographic characteristics. Ordinary least squares (OLS) regression analysis was employed to determine the proportion of variance in financial behaviors explained by the inclusion of the independent variables (viz., financial knowledge, attitude toward finances, and socio-demographic characteristics). As specified a priori, significant predictor variables ($p < .05$) showing an association of .20 or greater were regressed on the dependent variable, financial behaviors. Tolerance statistics were computed to assess multicollinearity among independent variables (Mertler & Vanatta, 2013). The results showed that the tolerance values for the variables age (0.09) and dependent child (0.08) did not meet tolerance criteria, and were therefore excluded from subsequent multivariate analysis.

Results

Respondents' financial knowledge levels

Participants correctly answered just over half (51.4%) of the 23 questions regarding financial literacy ($M = 11.8$, $SD = 4.2$). Overall, respondents performed well on the basic arithmetic section (83.0% correct), but reported relatively low levels of knowledge about saving and borrowing (43.2% correct), and investment and risk (41.8% correct). Table 3 shows the results of bivariate analysis of financial knowledge. Differences in the level of financial literacy emerged among three characteristics: educational attainment, income level, and years of employment. Specifically, the level of financial literacy was higher for those with a high school diploma ($M = 12.9$, $SD = 4.2$) than for those without ($M = 11.6$, $SD = 4.2$), at $t(327) = 2.00$, $p < .05$. Those who earned more than $243 per month ($M = 12.9$, $SD = 4.6$) demonstrated a higher level of financial literacy than those earning $243 or less per month ($M = 11.2$, $SD = 3.8$, $t = 3.58$, $df = 327$, $p < .001$. In addition, participants employed for more than 5 years ($M = 12.4$, $SD = 4.5$) scored higher than those employed for 5 years or less ($M = 11.3$, $SD = 3.8$), at $t(327) = 2.37$, $p < .05$.

Attitude toward finances and source of financial knowledge

With regard to attitude toward money management, about two-thirds (67.1%) believed managing money was necessary regardless of their financial situation. Less than 1 in 10 participants (7.9%) believed that managing money was necessary only when they had lots of money, whereas 35 participants (17.0%) reported that money management was necessary only when

Table 3. Results of bivariate analysis on financial knowledge.

Characteristics		Mean of numbers of correct answers	t
Gender	Male	12.8	1.31
	Female	12.2	
Age	23-year-old or younger	11.73	−0.49
	> 23 years	11.96	
Marital status	Single	12.05	1.15
	Married	11.5	
Children	No	12.85	1.86
	Yes	11.92	
Educational level	high school diploma or above	12.9	2.00*
	Less than high school diploma	11.6	
Monthly income	More than $243	12.9	3.58***
	$243 or less	11.2	
Years of employment	More than 5 years	12.4	2.37*
	5 years or less	11.3	

Note: $df = 327$, $p < 0.10$, $*p < 0.05$, $**p < 0.01$, $p < 0.001***$

they had limited financial resources. A slightly smaller proportion ($n = 47$, 14.2%) believed that making money was more important than managing money. Migrant workers earning more than $243 per month were significantly more likely to demonstrate a favorable attitude (i.e., managing money is necessary regardless of how much money you have), than those earning $243 or less, at λ^2 (1, 328) = 4.13, $p < .05$.

The largest proportions of participants reported that the primary sources of financial knowledge were family and friends (46.6%), social media (37.8%), and personal experience (35.3%). Only 25 out of 328 (7.6%) participants reported learning financial knowledge from formal financial institutions, whereas 50 (15.2%) participants gained this knowledge as part of their schooling. A similar proportion of participants ($n = 45$, 13.7%) learned financial knowledge from the internet. The same proportion of participants reported that the most reliable (42.2%) and beneficial (42.2%) source of financial knowledge was personal experience.

Respondents' financial behaviors

Participants reported that they engaged in half (51.0%) of the five beneficial financial behaviors ($M = 2.56$, $SD = 1.2$). Most participants reported keeping track of money (72.0%) and saving money for emergency (65.9%); however, less than one-third (28.5%) reported having a budget and only one-third (35.5%) had begun saving for retirement. Just over half of participants (54.1%) reported making ends meet. The results of correlational analyses showed that financial knowledge and behaviors were positively and weakly associated ($r = 0.26$, $p < .05$). OLS regression results showed that financial knowledge, attitude toward money management, and socio-demographic variables explained approximately 16–19% of the variance in financial behaviors, $F(8, 290) = 7.98$, $R^2 = .19$,

Table 4. Summary of multiple regression analysis for variables predicting financial behaviors ($N = 329$).

Variables	Coefficient	Standard Error	t	Sig
(Constant)	.19	.47	0.40	.68
Financial Knowledge	.04*	.02	2.34	.02
Financial Attitude	.64***	.14	4.45	.00
Gender	.02	.14	0.15	.88
Marital Status	.40*	.20	2.02	.04
Educational Level	−.13	.19	−0.69	.49
Monthly Income	.39*	.15	2.50	.01
Years of Employment	−.03	.16	−0.21	.84

Model Statistics: $R^2 = .19$ $R^2_{adj} = .16$, $F(8, 281) = 7.98$, $p < .0001$).
*$p < .05$, **$p < .01$, ***$p < .001$

$R^2_{adj} = .16$, $p < .001$. Among predictors, financial knowledge ($\beta = .04$, $p < .05$), attitude ($\beta = .64$, $p < .001$), income ($\beta = .39$, $p < .05$), and marital status ($\beta = .40$, $p < .05$) were positively associated with beneficial financial behaviors (See Table 4). Residual scatterplots were examined, revealing no violations of multiple regression assumptions of linearity, normality, and homoscedasticity (Tabachnik & Fidell, 2012).

Discussion

This study examined the financial knowledge and behaviors of rural-to-urban migrant workers, an understudied and financially at-risk subpopulation of the Chinese workforce. Overall, participants showed low levels of financial knowledge (51.4%). Although methodological differences across studies preclude meaningful comparison, the lack of adequate financial knowledge demonstrated by migrant workers in the current study is consistent with findings of previous research undertaken with other low-paid and less educated samples of workers (e.g., OECD, 2005; Zhan et al., 2006). Low levels of financial knowledge may further exacerbate Chinese migrant workers' already disadvantaged economic circumstances. For example, without a clear understanding of the relationship between rate-of-return and investment risk, Chinese migrant workers may unwittingly entrust their meager financial resources to exploitive entities, such as underground banks (Lusardi, 2013). Unaware of the difference between simple and compound interest, Chinese migrant workers may inadvertently forfeit the higher interest rates associated with certain types of savings accounts. The extant research has consistently shown a relationship between financial knowledge and financial decision making (Babiarz & Robb, 2014; Lusardi, 2013). Given the economic marginalization of Chinese migrant workers (Wong et al., 2007) and the absence of social welfare policies in place to protect them (Chen et al., 2010), the low levels of financial knowledge demonstrated by respondents in this study may render them especially vulnerable to the deleterious consequences of poor financial decision making.

Consistent with previous research (Hilgert et al., 2003; Song, 2011), higher levels of financial knowledge among participants in this study were associated with greater amounts of beneficial financial behaviors. In other words, individuals who were knowledgeable about effective money-management practices are more likely to report engaging in financially responsible behaviors. Conversely, it may also be true that migrant workers who behave in financially responsible ways may experience greater exposure to new sources of financial information, which could then bolster their money-management knowledge and skills. Given the cross-sectional design, it is beyond the scope of this study to examine the complex causal processes underlying the relationship between financial knowledge and financial behaviors. The body of intervention research in the field has yielded mixed results (see, e.g., Collins & O' Rourke, 2012; Rothwell & Sultana, 2013), in that financial education programs do not consistently achieve significant and positive outcomes regarding financial behaviors and subsequent wellbeing. The causal mechanism between financial knowledge and behaviors is unclear. Research with rigorous design and larger and more diverse samples are needed to further assess the impact of financial knowledge on financial behaviors and long-term wellbeing.

Although there was little variability in participants' income in this study, earning a higher income was associated with greater amounts of financially responsible behaviors. This is consistent with previous research demonstrating a positive association between income and responsible financial practices (e.g., Lusardi & Mitchell, 2007; Tang & Lachance, 2012). Thus, the findings underscore the importance of having financial resources available to take advantage of opportunities to engage in beneficial financial behaviors. This suggests a possible, additional source of vulnerability among Chinese migrant workers: Those with very limited financial resources are exposed to fewer opportunities to learn effective money management practices. Married migrant workers in this study reported a greater amount of financially responsible behaviors than did single workers, suggesting that those with families may be more motivated than their unmarried counterparts to engage in responsible financial practices. However, although results showed that the vast majority of married respondents had children (94.4%), information about the number of children was not collected; a potentially relevant predictor of migrant workers' financial behaviors that warrants inclusion in future research.

Results further showed that having a favorable attitude toward finances was associated with self-reported financially responsible behaviors. It is reasonable to assume that individuals who recognize the importance of managing money are more likely to engage in responsible financial practices than those who do not see the relevance of effective money management. However, few studies have examined whether workers' attitudes toward finances are related to financial literacy (e.g., MacFarland, Marconi, & Utkus, 2003; Turner, Bailey, & Scott, 1994). Thus, the findings of this study underscore the importance of assessing attitude as a potentially relevant predictor of Chinese migrant workers' financial practices in future research.

Finally, results showed that most respondents in this study relied on family, friends, and personal experience to obtain financial knowledge; although few reported receiving knowledge from formal sources such as school or financial institutions. This latter finding may reflect this population's limited access to formal financial educational opportunities; however, additional research is needed to determine the extent to which formal sources of financial knowledge actually are made available to rural migrant workers. Accurate information about migrant workers' access to formal financial knowledge is needed, given their socioeconomically marginalized status.

Implications for social work community practice and advocacy

The relatively low levels of financial knowledge demonstrated by the respondents in this study suggest that culturally-appropriate education, such as interventions that that teach money management skills, may be beneficial to Chinese migrant workers if such strategies are tailored to their unique socioeconomic circumstances. The study further showed that more favorable attitudes were associated with financially responsible behaviors. Thus, Chinese social workers in community practice settings should consider implementing culturally-sensitive outreach and community education strategies to promote migrant workers' awareness of and positive attitudes toward financial literacy. As Birkenmaier and Curley (2009) aptly observed, social workers who interact with financially disadvantaged populations on a regular basis are well positioned to link clients with available financial education resources and services. Rural migrant workers, however, earn low wages and are unlikely to have the resources to pay for professional financial counselling. Social workers engaged in outreach efforts should engage in empowerment-oriented practice and conduct culturally-relevant assessment, advocacy, and brokerage activities that can identify the financial literacy needs of Chinese migrant workers, as well as link them to existing community organizations and other institutions that support the financial and economic wellbeing of socioeconomically disadvantaged groups.

Rural-to-urban migrant workers have endured harsh socioeconomic conditions for 2 decades. Over the past few years, community organizations that support the rights of migrant workers have advocated for wage equality and improved working conditions (Chan, 2012). However, given the persistence of existing structural inequalities, these latter efforts are insufficient for addressing migrant workers' disparate access to employment opportunities, public services, health care, and other social welfare entitlements (Cheng et al., 2014; Song & Appleton, 2008). From a social justice perspective, this study underscores the timeliness and importance of needed state-initiated policy changes that could better the financial circumstances of Chinese migrant workers. Living an economically marginalized existence, migrant workers are often unable to give voice to concerns about their community (Wong et al., 2007). This points to the need for social work researchers and practitioners to advocate for this disfranchised population at the policy level. For example, as China moves to a more domestic, consumption-driven economy, ongoing reforms to the *hukou* policy are needed to facilitate greater economic participation of Chinese families (Lu, 2008; Ngok, 2012). Opportunities to engage in beneficial financial practices are more available to those with sufficient financial resources (O'Neil, Xiao, Bristow, Brennan, & Kerbel, 2000); therefore providing modest financial incentives that encourage and reinforce responsible money management (e.g., saving for emergencies, saving for retirement) is a policy-practice approach that could target migrant workers' inherent economic vulnerability. Lessons can be learned, for example, from the Individual Development Account (IDA) program in the United States, which provides financial assistance in the form of financial incentives (i.e., asset building) and education to low-income populations. The IDA programs have been successful in improving the financial knowledge and behaviors of financially at-risk workers (Birkenmaier, Curley, & Kelly, 2012; Im & Busette, 2010). In conjunction with other efforts to reform the oppressive *hukou* system, social workers in China should play an active role implementing and testing similar financial incentive programs to better assist rural-to-urban migrants and other economically vulnerable workers.

Limitations, merits, and conclusions

As with all exploratory-descriptive research, this study has several limitations that merit acknowledgement. First, a nonprobability sampling method was used to collect data; thus, the findings cannot be generalized to the broader population of Chinese migrant workers. In contrast with Xia et al.'s (2014) sample of city residents and Song's (2011) sample of rural residents, the sample of rural-to-urban migrant workers used in this study represents a substantially different population of Chinese workers with regard to key socio-demographic characteristics (e.g., age, educational attainment, income levels) and legal residency status. However, the lack of contextualized information about the on-campus setting makes it difficult to compare the results of the current study with those yielded in studies of migrant workers in other settings. Although it is difficult, if not impossible to utilize a probability sampling method to recruit Chinese migrant workers, Landry and Shen (2005) recommend employing a novel sampling strategy, such as spatial sampling, to obtain a reasonably representative sample of migrant workers (Landry & Shen, 2005).

There are also issues with measurement. Although the BFLS measure was pretested with a comparable population, its empirical validity has not been established. Additional reliability testing of the BFLS is needed with larger and more diverse samples of Chinese rural migrant workers. Using face-to-face interviews to collect the survey data is another potential measurement issue, in that participants may have provided biased responses to make themselves appear more financially responsible to the researcher. Thus, future research should verify self-reported financial behaviors and use measures that demonstrate good reliability and validity.

The final multivariate model in this study explained a rather modest portion of the variance in workers' financial behaviors, suggesting that additional influential correlates should be tested in future research. One variable of possible relevance is social connectedness, that is, workers' network of family and friends, which was the primary source of financial knowledge reported by almost half of respondents in this study. Previous research has underscored the importance of employees' personal network of family members and friends as a source of financial knowledge (e.g., Hilgert et al., 2003). Chinese rural migrant workers often rely heavily on family and friends to locate employment and housing in urban settings (NBSC, 2012); thus, in the absence of formal financial education, it is very likely that migrant workers' social networks play an influential role in their financial decision making and behaviors. Additional variables that may merit examination in future research with rural migrant workers include number of dependents, length of current residence, length of time with current employer, and number of years employed in cities. These latter variables are concerned with stability in living arrangements, an especially relevant issue for Chinese migrant workers (NBSC, 2012).

Despite its limitations, this study is the first known study to examine the financial knowledge, attitudes, and behaviors of urban-to-rural Chinese migrant workers, a unique subset of low-paid Chinese workers. It builds upon existing knowledge by incorporating the BFLS to assess financial literacy as a comprehensive and multidimensional construct, and by including variables that have emerged as relevant predictors of financial behaviors in previous research. The findings highlight migrant workers' low levels of financial knowledge, and demonstrated associations between financially responsible behaviors and financial knowledge, attitudes, and marital status. Although reforms are underway in China, the *hukou* registration policy is a longstanding barrier that has prevented migrant workers from accessing stable employment, job-related benefits, and public services

(Chen et al., 2010). However, having accurate financial knowledge may serve to mitigate migrant workers' inherent economic vulnerability, better positioning them to avoid fraudulent practices and to take advantage of available economic opportunities and publicly funded insurance programs. Making culturally-relevant financial education available to Chinese migrant workers' may be an effective policy tool for promoting the social integration of migrant workers into local communities, an approach that has been used in other countries (e.g., Lutheran Immigration and Refugee Services, 2006). This study provides preliminary information about the financial literacy of Chinese migrant workers. Additional, descriptive research is needed to assess interrelationships among financial literacy and relevant environmental and social variables, as well as longitudinal research that examines the consequences of workers' financial decision-making processes.

References

Allgood, S., & Walstad, W. (2011). *The effects of perceived and actual financial knowledge on credit card behavior* (NFI Working Paper No.15). Terre Haute, IN: Networks Financial Institute. Retrieved from http://indstate.edu/business/nfi/leadership/papers/2011-WP-15_Walstad_Allgood.pdf

Atkinson, A., McKay, S., Kempson, E., & Collard, S. (2006, March). *Levels of financial capability in the UK: Results of a baseline survey*. Bristol, UK: Financial Services Authority. Retrieved from http://www.fsa.gov.uk/pubs/consumer-research/crpr47.pdf

Babiarz, P., & Robb, C. A. (2014). Financial literacy and emergency saving. *Journal of Family and Economic Issues, 35*(1), 40–50. doi:10.1007/s10834-013-9369-9

Beal, D. J., & Delpachitra, S. B. (2003). Financial literacy among Australian university students. *Economic Papers, 22*(1), 65–78.

Bernheim, D. (1998). Financial illiteracy, education and retirement saving. In O. Mitchell, & S. Schieber (Eds.), *Living with defined contribution pensions* (pp. 38–68). Philadelphia, MA: University of Pennsylvania Press.

Birkenmaier, J., & Curley, J. (2009). Financial credit: Social work's role in empowering low-income families. *Journal of Community Practice, 17*(3), 251–268. doi:10.1080/10705420903117973

Birkenmaier, J., Curley, J., & Kelly, P. (2012). Credit building in IDA programs: Early findings of a longitudinal study. *Research on Social Work Practice, 22*(6), 605–614. doi:10.1177/1049731512453208

Bowen, C. F. (2002). Financial knowledge of teens and their parents. *Financial Counseling and Planning, 13*(2), 93–102.

Caratelli, M., & Ricci, O. (2011). *The relationship between everyday practices and financial literacy: An empirical analysis* (Working Paper No. 37114). Retrieved from https://mpra.ub.uni-muenchen.de/37114/1/MPRA_paper_37114.pdf

Chan, C. K. (2012). Community-based organizations for migrant workers' rights: The emergence of labour NGOs in China. *Community Development Journal, 48*(1), 6–22. doi:10.1093/cdj/bss001

Chang, Y., & Lyons, A. (2007). *Are financial education programs meeting the needs of financially disadvantaged consumers?* (NFI Working Paper No. 02). Terre Haute, IN: Networks Financial Institute.

Chen, B., Lu, M., & Zhong, N. (2015). How urban segregation distorts Chinese migrants' consumption? *World Development, 70*, 133–146. doi:10.1016/j.worlddev.2014.11.019

Chen, C., Lucas, H., Bloom, G., & Ding, S. (2010, September). *Internal migration and 'rural/urban' households in China: Implication for health care.* Paper produced for the Conference Ten Years of War against Poverty, Manchester, UK.

Chen, H., & Volpe, R. (1998). An analysis of personal financial literacy among college students. *Financial Services Review, 7*(2), 107–128. doi:10.1016/S1057-0810(99)80006-7

Chen, H., & Volpe, R. P. (2002). Gender differences in personal financial literacy among college students. *Financial Services Review, 11*(3), 289–307.

Cheng, Z., Nielsen, I., & Smyth, R. (2014). Access to social insurance in urban China: A comparative study of rural-urban and urban-urban migrants in Beijing. *Habitat International, 41*, 243–252. doi:10.1016/j.habitatint.2013.08.007

Collins, J. M., & O'Rourke, C. (2012). *Still holding out promise: A review of financial literacy education and financial counselling studies* (Working Paper NO. 02). Terre Haute, IN: Networks Financial Institute.

Danes, S. M., & Haberman, H. (2004). Evaluation of the NEFE high school financial planning program: 2003-04. *National Endowment for Financial Education.* Retrieved from http://www.hsfpp.org/Portals/0/Documents/NEFE%20HSFPP%20Impact%20Study%202003-2004.pdf

De Brauw, A., & Giles, J. T. (2012). *Migrant labor markets and the welfare of rural households in the developing world: Evidence from China* (IZA Discussion Paper No. 6765). Bonn, Germany: Institution for the Study of Labor (IZA). Retrieved from http://papers.ssrn.com/sol3/papers.cfm?abstract_id=2157907

De Brauw, A., & Rozelle, S. (2008). Migration and household investment in rural China. *China Economic Review, 19*(2), 320–335. doi:10.1016/j.chieco.2006.10.004

Financial Industry Regulatory Authority. (2003). *NASD investor literacy research: Executive summary.* New York, NY: Applied Research & Consulting LLC. Retrieved from http://www.finra.org/web/groups/investors/@inv/@protect/documents/investors/p011459.pdf

Garman, E. T., & Forgue, R. E. (2014). *Personal finance* (12th ed.). Boston, MA: Cengage Learning.

Garman, E. T., Leech, I. E., & Grable, J. E. (1997). The negative impact of employee poor personal financial behaviors on employees. *Financial Counseling and Planning, 7*, 157–167.

Giles, J., & Yoo, K. (2007). Precautionary behavior, migrant networks, and household consumption decisions: An empirical analysis using household panel data from rural China. *The Review of Economics and Statistics, 89*(3), 534–551. doi:10.1162/rest.89.3.534

Goldsmith, R. E., & Goldsmith, E. B. (2006). The effects of investment education on gender differences in financial knowledge. *Journal of Personal Finance, 5*(2), 55–69.

Hilgert, M. A., Hogarth, J. M., & Beverly, S. G. (2003). Household financial management: The connection between knowledge and behavior. *Federal Reserve Bulletin, 89*(7), 311–323.

Hogarth, J. M., & Hilgert, M. A. (2002). Financial knowledge, experience and learning preferences: Preliminary results from a new survey on financial literacy. *Consumer Interests Annual, 48*, 1–7.

Hung, A. A., Parker, A. M., & Yoong, J. (2009). *Defining and measuring financial literacy* (Working Paper No.708). Santa Monica, CA: RAND Labor and Population.

Huston, S. J. (2010). Measuring financial literacy. *Journal of Consumer Affairs, 44*(2), 296–316. doi:10.1111/j.1745-6606.2010.01170.x

Im, L., & Busette, C. M. (2010). *What motivates low income earners to save money?* EARN Research Brief. San Francisco, CA: EARN Research Institute.

Jump$tart Coalition for Personal Financial Literacy (Jump$tart). (2007). *National standards in K-12 personal finance education.* Retrieved from http://www.jumpstart.org/assets/files/2015_NationalStandardsBook.pdf

Kempson, E., Collard, S., Turtle, J., & Worley, A. (2006, March). *Financial capability baseline survey: Questionnaire.* Bristol, UK: Financial Services Authority.

Kindle, P. A. (2010). Student perceptions of financial literacy: Relevance to practice. *Journal of Social Service Research, 36*(5), 470–481. doi:10.1080/01488376.2010.510951

Landry, P. F., & Shen, M. (2005). Reaching migrants in survey research: The use of the global positioning system to reduce coverage bias in China. *Policy Analysis, 13*, 1–22.

Loke, V., & Hageman, S. A. (2013). Debt literacy and social work. *Journal of Financial Therapy, 4*(1), 63–82. doi:10.4148/jft.v4i1.1795

Lu, Y. (2008). Does hukou still matter? The household registration system and its impact on social stratification and mobility in China. *Social Sciences in China, 29*, 56–75. doi:10.1080/02529200802091250

Lusardi, A. (2008). *Financial literacy: An essential tool for informed consumer choice?* (Working Paper No. 14084). Retrieved from http://www.econstor.eu/bitstream/10419/25554/1/577553798.PDF

Lusardi, A. (2013). *Financial literacy and high-cost borrowing in the United States* (NBER Working Paper No. 18969). Retrieved from http://www.nber.org/papers/w18969

Lusardi, A., & Mitchell, O. S. (2005). *Financial literacy and planning: Implication for retirement wellbeing* (Research Paper No. 108). Retrieved from http://papers.ssrn.com/sol3/papers.cfm?abstract_id=881847

Lusardi, A., & Mitchell, O. S. (2007). *Financial literacy and retirement: New evidence from the Rand American Life Panel* (Research Report No. 157). Ann Arbor, MI: University of Michigan Retirement Research Center.

Lusardi, A., & Mitchell, O. S. (2008). Planning and financial literacy: How do women fare? *American Economic Review: Papers & Proceedings, 98*, 413–417. doi:10.1257/aer.98.2.413

Lusardi, A., & Mitchell, O. S. (2011). *Financial literacy and planning: Implications for retirement wellbeing.* Cambridge, MA: National Bureau of Economic Research.

Lutheran Immigration and Refugee Services. (2006). *Financial literacy for newcomers: Weaving immigrant needs into financial education.* Baltimore, MD: Lutheran Immigration and Refugee Services.

Lyons, A. C., Chang, Y., & Scherpf, E. M. (2006). Translating financial education into behavior change for low-income populations. *Financial Counseling and Planning, 17*(2), 27–45.

MacFarland, D. M., Marconi, C. D., & Utkus, S. P. (2003). *Money attitudes and retirement plan design: One size does not fit all* (PRC Working Paper 2003-11). Philadelphia, PA: Pensions Research Council. Retrieved from http://citeseerx.ist.psu.edu/viewdoc/download?doi=10.1.1.198.9360&rep=rep1&type=pdf

Mandell, L. (2006). *Financial literacy: If it's so important, why isn't it improving?* (NFI Working Paper NO. 08). Terre Haute, IN: Networks Financial Institute. Retrieved from http://www.isunetworks.com/pdfs/profiles/2006-PB-08_Mandell.pdf

Mertler, C. A., & Vannatta, R. A. (2013). *Advanced and multivariate statistical methods: Practical application and interpretation* (5th ed.). Glendale, CA: Pyrczak.

Moore, D. (2003). *Survey of financial literacy in Washington State: Knowledge, behavior, attitudes, and experiences* (Report No. 39). Washington, DC: Social and Economic Sciences Research Center.

National Bureau of Statistics of China. (2012). *Report on China's migrant population: 2012.* Beijing, China: National Bureau of Statistics of China. Retrieved from http://www.stats.gov.cn/tjsj/zxfb/201305/t20130527_12978.html

National Council on Economic Education. (2005). *What American teens & adults know about economics.* Rochester, NY: Harris Interactive. Retrieved from http://www.councilforeconed.org/cel/WhatAmericansKnowAboutEconomics_042605-3.pdf

National Financial Capability Study. (2009). *Financial capability in the United States: National survey-executive summary.* Washington, DC: FINRA Investor Education Foundation.

Ngok, K. (2012). Serving migrant workers: A challenging public service issue in China. *Australian Journal of Public Administration, 71*(2), 178–190. doi:10.1111/j.1467-8500.2012.00761.x

O'Neill, B., Xiao, J. J., Bristow, B., Brennan, P., & Kerbel, C. M. (2000). Successful financial goal attainment: Perceived resources and obstacles. *Financial Counseling and Planning, 11*(1), 1–12.

Organization for Economic Co-operation and Development. (2005). *Improving financial literacy: Analysis of issues and policies.* Paris, France: Author.

Perry, V. G., & Morris, M. D. (2005). Who is in control? The role of self-perception, knowledge, and income in explaining consumer financial behavior. *Journal of Consumer Affairs, 39*(2), 299–313. doi:10.1111/joca.2005.39.issue-2

Remund, D. L. (2010). Financial literacy explicated: The case for a clearer definition in an increasingly complex economy. *Journal of Consumer Affairs, 44*(2), 276–295. doi:10.1111/j.1745-6606.2010.01169.x

Rothwell, D., & Sultana, N. (2013). Cash-flow and savings practices of low-income households: Evidence from a follow-up study of IDA participants. *Journal of Social Service Research, 39*(2), 281–292. doi:10.1080/01488376.2012.754828

Servon, L. J., & Kaestner, R. (2008). Consumer financial literacy and the impact of online banking on the financial behavior of lower income bank customers. *Journal of Consumer Affairs, 42*(2), 271–305. doi:10.1111/j.1745-6606.2008.00108.x

Song, C. (2011). *Financial illiteracy and pension contributions: A field experiment on compound interest in China* (Unpublished paper). Retrieved from http://works.bepress.com/changcheng_song/1/

Song, L., & Appleton, S. (2008). Social protection and migration in China: What can protect migrants from economic uncertainty? In I. Nielson, & R. Smyth (Eds.), *Migration and social protection in China* (pp. 138–154). Singapore: World Scientific.

Tabachnik, B. G., & Fidell, L. S. (2012). *Using multivariate statistics* (6th ed.). Upper Saddle River, NJ: Pearson.

Tang, N., & Lachance, M. E. (2012). Financial advice: What about low-income consumers? *Journal of Personal Finance, 11*(2), 121–158.

Taylor, J. E., Rozelle, S., & De Brauw, A. (2003). Migration and incomes in source communities: A new economics of migration perspective from China. *Economic Development and Cultural Change, 52*(1), 75–101. doi:10.1086/380135

Turner, M. J., Bailey, W. C., & Scott, J. P. (1994). Factors influencing attitude toward retirement and retirement planning among midlife university employees. *Journal of Applied Gerontology, 13*(2), 143–156. doi:10.1177/073346489401300203

Van Rooij, M., Lusardi, A., & Alessie, R. (2011). Financial literacy and stock market participation. *Journal of Financial Economics, 101*(2), 449–472. doi:10.1016/j.jfineco.2011.03.006

Vitt, L. A., Anderson, C., Kent, J., Lyter, D. M., Siegenthaler, J. K., & Ward, J. (2000). *Personal finance and the rush to competence: Financial literacy education in the U.S.* Middleburg, VA: Institute for Socio-Financial Studies.

Volpe, R. P., Chen, H., & Liu, S. (2006). An analysis of the importance of personal finance topics and the level of knowledge possessed by working adults. *Financial Services Review*, *15*(1), 81–98.

Volpe, R. P., Chen, H., & Pavlicko, J. J. (1996). Personal investment literacy among college students: A survey. *Financial Practice and Education*, *6*(2), 86–94.

Wong, K., Fu, D., Li, C. Y., & Song, H. X. (2007). Rural migrant workers in urban China: Living a marginalized life. *International Journal of Social Welfare*, *16*(1), 32–40. doi:10.1111/j.1468-2397.2007.00475.x

Worthington, A. C. (2006). Predicting financial literacy in Australia. *Financial Services Review*, *15*(1), 59–79. Retrieved from http://works.bepress.com/acworthington/38

Xia, T., Wang, Z., & Li, K. (2014). Financial literacy overconfidence and stock market participation. *Social Indicators Research*, *119*, 1233–1245. doi:10.1007/s11205-013-0555-9

Xiao, J. J. (2008). Applying behavior theories to financial behavior. In J. J. Xiao (Ed.), *Handbook of consumer finance research* (pp. 69–81). New York, NY: Springer.

Xu, L., & Zia, B. (2013). *Financial literacy around the world: An overview of the evidence with practical suggestions for the way forward* (World Bank Working Paper No. 6107). Washington, DC: World Bank. Retrieved from http://papers.ssrn.com/sol3/papers.cfm?abstract_id=2248863

Xu, Q., Guan, X., & Yao, F. (2011). Welfare program participation among rural-to-urban migrant workers in China. *International Journal of Social Welfare*, *20*(1), 10–21. doi:10.1111/j.1468-2397.2009.00713.x

Yu, K. M., Wu, A. M., Chan, W. S., & Chou, K. L. (2015). Gender differences in financial literacy among Hong Kong workers. *Educational Gerontology*, *41*(4), 315–326. doi:10.1080/03601277.2014.966548

Zhan, M., Anderson, S. G., & Scott, J. (2006). Financial management knowledge of the low-income population. *Journal of Social Service Research*, *33*(1), 93–106. doi:10.1300/J079v33n01_09

Zhu, Y., Wu, Z., Wang, M., Du, Y., & Cai, F. (2012). Do migrants really save more? Understanding the impact of remittances on savings in rural China. *Journal of Development Studies*, *48*(5), 654–672. doi:10.1080/00220388.2011.638141

Index

INDEX

INDEX

For Product Safety Concerns and Information please contact our EU
representative GPSR@taylorandfrancis.com
Taylor & Francis Verlag GmbH, Kaufingerstraße 24, 80331 München, Germany

www.ingramcontent.com/pod-product-compliance
Ingram Content Group UK Ltd.
Pitfield, Milton Keynes, MK11 3LW, UK
UKHW051831180425
457613UK00022B/1192